A Plan
for Writing

A Plan for Writing

JOHN C. BRERETON

Queensborough Community College
of The City University of New York

HOLT, RINEHART AND WINSTON
New York   Chicago   San Francisco   Atlanta
Dallas   Montreal   Toronto

To Ginny

Library of Congress Cataloging in Publication Data

Brereton, John C.
  A plan for writing.
  Includes index.
    1. English language—Rhetoric. I. Title.
PR1408.B679   808'.042   77–12803
ISBN: 0-03-019516-0

Preface

A Plan for Writing is meant for beginning college writers, students who need to improve their English skills as quickly as possible. Most of these students—most of all students, in fact—did not excel in high school composition and rarely enjoyed the challenge of writing or the satisfaction that its mastery can bring. This book deals with the situation by providing the fundamentals of rhetoric (Chapters 1–3) and the elements of a good written English (Chapters 4–8). At the end of a semester, students should be able to write well-organized four- to six-paragraph essays that display skill in the basics of grammar, mechanics, and usage.

The book moves from short descriptive paragraphs to longer expository essays. The progression is swift, reflecting my belief that students benefit most from the challenge of organizational problems at the outset. Rhetorical strategies and refinements are treated in the context of the full essay, ensuring that the methods of developing an idea will arise in a meaningful manner because the class will have been facing this issue almost from the beginning of the semester.

The chapters on grammar, mechanics, and word choice are grouped together in the order of their importance, but they are all independent units that may be given in any order desirable or necessary. Indeed, the flexible format of the book makes it entirely possible to begin the course with work on individual sentences and then proceed to paragraph and essay structure. Three possible orders for teaching are supplied in the Instructor's Manual that accompanies the text. None of them requires any major rearrangement of the text, for few chapters depend on other chapters. The Manual may be obtained through a local Holt representative or by writing to: English Editor, College Department, Holt, Rinehart and Winston, 383 Madison Avenue, New York, N.Y. 10017.

The instructor should note at the outset that this book does not aim to be comprehensive. There is nothing on the subtleties of plural possession or the use of the dash; beginning college writers need intensive work on organization, paragraph development, and sentence structure first. At the same time, students will not find a rehash of traditional grammar. Grammatical terms are mentioned, but their use is purposely kept to a bare minimum. When a grammatical explanation is necessary, it is provided; when a point can be made without grammar getting in the way, I have not hesitated to excise the unnecessary terminology. I believe that students do not learn to write by learning grammar, but that some grammar is a necessary appendage to many important writing skills. Usage and mechanics are treated as important subsidiaries of the main part of the course—the production of clear and thoughtful essays.

Finally, this book incorporates extensive work in sentence combining, a promising technique that can, if used properly, make important changes in student writing. The long chapter on combining sentences, "Toward Mature Sentences," provides all necessary directions; it is also keyed to relevant chapters on sentence structure and style. The attempt in the combining exercises—in all the exercises throughout the book—is to have students generate sentences of their own. Once a skill is taught, there is an opportunity to try it out immediately. The tests usually involve writing real sentences, not simply picking out one of two boxed alternatives on a multiple-choice test. *A Plan for Writing* makes the students write out almost every answer and then apply the lesson at once to their own compositions.

I wish to thank the following who made helpful criticisms and suggestions about the manuscript: Professors Robert Brown, University of Maryland; Ken Burrows, West Virginia Institute of Technology; Charles Cobb, Los Angeles Pierce College; Teresa Glazier, Western Illinois University; George Gleason, Southwest Missouri State University; Dixie Goswami, Middlesex County College; James Peck, Jefferson State Junior College; David Skwire, Cuyahoga Community College; and Marilyn Sternglass, Indiana University of Pennsylvania.

One of an author's most pleasant tasks is to acknowledge help from colleagues and friends. It is clear to me that without the students and faculty of Queensborough's Basic Skills Department this book would never have been written. Jerrold Nudelman offered encouragement even before the book was begun, and he, along with Manette Berlinger, Charles Martin, and Lynn Troyka, supplied sound criticism of an early draft. One could not ask for more responsive colleagues. Finally, the originators of some specific methods and approaches ought to receive credit: Frank O'Hare for help in sentence combining and punctuation; Mina Shaughnessy for ideas on paragraph development; and Lynn Troyka for suggestions on capitalization. Needless to say, I take full responsibility for the way I have adapted their work.

J.C.B.

Contents

A Plan
for Writing

CHAPTER 1

FROM PARAGRAPH TO ESSAY

The Paragraph

A paragraph is simply a group of sentences about a single main idea or point. The sentences that form the paragraph all contribute to the point; they make it more complete and understandable than any single sentence could.

It helps to think of paragraphs in relation to conversation. The same point that could be made in a conversation between two people would look very different as a written paragraph.

CONVERSATION

Jean: I had a terrible job last summer.
Jan: You did?
Jean: Yes. I worked as a toll collector on the Callahan Tunnel. It was awful.
Jan: What was so awful about it?
Jean: It was boring. All I did was reach out and collect fifty cents from every driver. If somebody didn't have change, I'd supply it.
Jan: What was so bad about that?
Jean: I had to spend eight hours a day cramped up in a stifling toll booth sticking my arm out to collect money. It was so dull.

Jan: I see.

Jean: And I never had a chance to talk to anybody. The most I'd do was give directions, and then the cars in line would start beeping their horns.

Jan: I see.

Jean: Another bad part was the exhaust fumes. The air at the tunnel entrance was full of smoke and pollution all summer. It got so bad I could hardly breathe after a couple of hours, yet I still had to stand there and stick my arm out.

Jan: But I bet the money was good.

Jean: No, it was terrible.

Jan: How much did you get?

Jean: Peanuts.

Jan: No, really, how much did you get?

Jean: Two-fifty an hour.

Jan: How much was that a week?

Jean: Let's see. Forty hours times two fifty, that's one hundred dollars a week.

Jan: Didn't you get overtime?

Jean: No, I didn't want any. Forty hours a week was enough for me. I couldn't stand it any more than that. I was so bored and choked by the pollution.

Jan: That's too bad.

Jean: Yes, I'll never take another job like that again.

WRITING

> I had a terrible job last summer. I worked as a toll collector on the Callahan Tunnel in downtown Boston. For eight hours a day I would stand in the little toll booth and stick out my arm and collect fifty cents from each passing car. It was so boring that I used to hope someone would hand me a big bill so I could make change. When someone asked me directions I would have a few seconds to chat before the cars in line started honking their horns. On top of the dullness of the job there were the unpleasant working conditions. My booth had no air conditioning, and the fumes from the cars combined with the summer heat made it difficult to breathe. The job wasn't worth the $2.50 an hour I earned. I'll never do it again.

In writing, Jean didn't have Jan to ask questions. Instead, Jean had to *anticipate* them and include the answers as explanations of what made the job so terrible. The result is a good paragraph that says just as much as the conversation, but in a different form.

There are two parts to Jean's paragraph about working as a toll collector: the *topic sentence* (often the first sentence, as here) and the rest of the sentences that explain what the job was like. The paragraph is good because it is <u>unified</u>. That is, every sentence is related to the topic sentence; the whole paragraph sticks to one subject. The topic sentence at the beginning makes a single point and the rest of the sentences back it up with explanation.

A paragraph must be about a single point.

---

6. A rock concert can be a whole new experience.
7. One day at the beach is worth ten days in the city.
8. A farm delights children.
9. My trip to _____showed me a way of life I had never seen before.
10. A meal at _____ is a memorable event.

The Essay

An essay is a group of paragraphs about a single point. An essay is longer than a single paragraph because the point it makes is more complex. Each separate paragraph of the essay explains some part of the essay's overall point. That is, the main idea of each paragraph helps prove the point the essay makes. Look at this example of a good student essay.

Does Crime Pay?

What do people mean when they say that crime does not pay? They probably mean that it doesn't pay if you're caught and locked up for a few years, and I agree. But not all criminals get caught. Some crimes are so profitable that many people are willing to take the risk.

If you consider committing a crime, you must figure the odds of getting caught. Not many crimes get solved by the police in the Kojak or Columbo fashion. When you look at the statistics, you see that about 50 percent of all crimes get solved. Certain acts of crime, of course, have higher odds of getting caught. Criminals are usually identified when they shoot somebody in the street or rob a bank. How can they expect to get away with it forever?

Crimes committed in business are much safer for someone who wants to get rich and stay out of jail. It requires more thinking to make the money dishonestly, but the rewards may be great. People who sell phony stock or steal from their employers also can get caught, but they could be let off easily. Some companies have been breaking the law for years, but when they get caught they may receive only tiny fines.

Small-time petty larceny and dope dealing are hard to control. There are so many opportunities to make money that the police cannot catch up with all criminals. Take selling marijuana; the chances of getting arrested for selling pot to your friends are about 50 to 1. This kind of crime can pay very well, but there is always the chance of going to jail.

Obviously there are crimes that do pay, and pay well. There is another side to the story, though, the moral side. Even if a criminal makes a good living from crime and never gets caught, he pays a moral price. Constant lying and cheating may make money, but they do not make for a good life or a clear conscience.

This essay has a single main point, or thesis; that is, some kinds of crime do pay well. Each of the middle three paragraphs helps explain how certain crimes might pay off. Then the conclusion draws the essay together by supplying a final thought that follows from what has been said earlier.

Another way to think of the essay is to diagram it.

Title

I	INTRODUCTION 2–5 sentences
II	MAIN BODY 5–8 sentences
III	MAIN BODY 5–8 sentences
IV	MAIN BODY 5–8 sentences
V	CONCLUSION 2–5 sentences

As the diagram shows, the essay has three main parts: an Introduction (paragraph I), the Main Body (paragrphs II, III, and IV), and a Conclusion (paragraph V). Each separate part has a distinct function:

Introduction (a) presents the subject to the reader. CREATES INTEREST
(b) states the point of the essay.

Main Body (a) explains your point.
(b) persuades the reader that you are right.

Conclusion (a) ends the discussion.
(b) leaves the reader thinking.

Think of the three main parts of an essay as the answers to these questions:
What's your point?   Introduction
How can you prove it?   Main Body
So what?   Conclusion

It is important to remember that the five-paragraph essay form is a guide, not a straitjacket. There will be times when you have four main points to make, so you will need four main-body paragraphs. Similarly, you might have a topic that calls for only two main-body paragraphs. Do not allow the five-paragraph form to force you into awkwardness. Simply think of it as a useful model.

GETTING STARTED: THE THESIS SENTENCE

One of the most difficult things to overcome when starting to write is fear of the blank page. Everyone, from the professional author to the beginning student is threatened at times by that empty piece of paper. But there are some techniques that can help you start your essay the right way.

First of all, of course, you *think* about your topic and what you know about it. Then you decide what the main point is. The best way to begin the essay is to write a *thesis sentence*, the one statement that expresses the main point of the whole essay. The following paragraphs will back up the thesis sentence by giving details that explain and prove it.

To develop a thesis sentence, ask yourself if you have any immediate reactions to the topic. Does the topic give you any associations? Do you know anything definite about it? Sometimes you don't have to think consciously; just sit back and let your mind play with the topic. If something strikes you as a possible thesis, put it in the form of a sentence and see how it sounds.

A thesis sentence must contain your opinion or attitude toward the topic. It will tell the reader your point of view, the trend your essay will take. The essay that opened this section, for instance, has a good thesis sentence:

> Some crimes are so profitable that many people are willing to take the risk.

The student who wrote this expressed a very clear opinion in her thesis sentence. She committed herself to showing how some crimes are very profitable but are often risky.

To see how you can compose a thesis sentence, watch how another student arrived at one for an essay on the subject of tennis. He tried to come up with a sentence that expressed an attitude or opinion *about the topic and nothing else*. He wrote:

A. I like tennis.
B. I like tennis because it is exciting.
C. I like to play tennis because it is exciting.

The third thesis sentence is much better than the first because it narrows the topic down to playing tennis instead of just "liking" it, which could include watching, playing, and reading about it.

The student then had a real thesis to explain, argue, and back up in the rest of the essay. He also could use his thesis sentence as a constant reminder to himself that his paragraphs would have to stick closely to the one main point of his essay. He could not wander off into anything else except explaining why playing tennis is exciting. The good thesis sentence helps keep the paper on its main point. Compare these two columns of thesis sentences. Those on the left are vague. Those on the right are specific and express an attitude or opinion.

Poor	Good
1. Some college students live at home while others live on campus.	1. College students get a better education when they live on campus.
2. There are several great advantages to television.	2. Television news has brought the whole world into our living rooms.
3. Living in the country has its good points.	3. Life in the rural Northwest puts people in touch with the world around them.

EXERCISE 14

Improve these poor thesis sentences:

1. Being overweight is bad.   _____

   _____

2. Professor Sen was a good teacher.   _____

   _____

3. Having a sense of humor has its advantages.   _____

   _____

4. The car of the future will be different.   _____

   _____

5. Novels make good reading.   _____

   _____

EXERCISE 15

Write *two* thesis sentences about each of the following topics. This means that you will have to narrow down the topic one way in the first thesis sentence and narrow it down in another, different, way in the second. The first one is done for you.

1. *Topic:* _____is my favorite place.
   Thesis sentence A: My cabin in the Sierras is the most peaceful place in the world.
   Thesis sentence B: My Aunt Nell's house is where I enjoy myself the most in the summertime.

2. *Topic:* The best possible job is _____.

   Thesis sentence A: _____

   _____

   _____

   Thesis sentence B: _____

   _____

   _____

3. *Topic:* Conserving energy is everyone's responsibility.

   Thesis sentence A: _____

   _____

   _____

   Thesis sentence B: _____

   _____

   _____

4. *Topic:* High schools ought to make learning more fun.

   Thesis sentence A: _____

   _____

   _____

   Thesis sentence B: _____

   _____

   _____

5. *Topic:* _____ is the best time of year.

   Thesis sentence A: _____

   _____

   _____

   Thesis sentence B: _____

   _____

   _____

Other Methods of Arriving at a Thesis Sentence

If you are having trouble thinking of a good thesis sentence, try these approaches:

1. Start writing on the topic for 5 minutes. Don't stop for anything; don't

even put your pen down. After the 5 minutes are up, look over what you've written. Most of it will be garbage, but somewhere in all the junk there may be an idea, an attitude, an issue, a notion. That's what you are looking for. Write it out in the form of a sentence and see if it sounds like the thesis you want. If you have enough information about it, it's good.

2. Jot down five or six very specific reactions to the topic. What does the topic mean to you? What comes into your mind? Be as specific as you can, but don't worry about the quality of the writing. You are looking for a sharp reaction, a real point of view. If you can put your reaction in the form of a sentence and write an essay on it, that's your thesis sentence.

3. Ask: "What do I really know about this topic?" or "What do I believe about it?" Make a list of what you know and believe; be detailed. Does the list give you a direction to move in? Does it show you where your attitudes and opinions are? If so, write out a sentence that sums up what you think. That's your thesis sentence.

Once you have a thesis sentence you are ready to begin writing. The best place for the thesis sentence is usually the last sentence of the introduction. When placed there, the thesis sentence sets up in the reader's mind the point you want to make, and then immediately hits him with a supporting detail in the main body paragraph that follows.

Paragraph	Essay
Topic sentence	*Thesis sentence*
The opening sentence	The last sentence of the introductory paragraph
Provides unity for the paragraph	Provides unity for the essay
Every sentence in the paragraph will back it up	Every paragraph in the essay will back it up

THE MAIN BODY PARAGRAPHS

A paragraph is a group of sentences about one particular point or main idea. Since you will usually be writing three main body paragraphs in your essays, you will obviously need to have three distinctly different points to make. Each one of your three main body paragraphs will be about one particular aspect of the essay's thesis sentence.

Example

Here is a rough outline of an essay about raising tomatoes.

Par. I.
Thesis sentence

INTRODUCTION
Raising tomatoes requires careful attention.

Par. II.

Tomatoes need good soil and plenty of fertilizer.

Abstract language tends to deal with broad categories; it covers a wide area instead of concentrating on precise, observable details. When you write about "human beings," you are being general; when you write about "Bernie Atkins," you are being specific.

How do you go about breaking down an abstract thought into its specific parts? Let's start with the abstract word "universe":

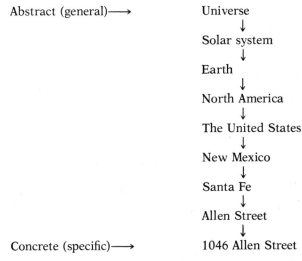

Abstract (general) ⟶

Universe
↓
Solar system
↓
Earth
↓
North America
↓
The United States
↓
New Mexico
↓
Santa Fe
↓
Allen Street
↓
1046 Allen Street

Concrete (specific) ⟶

In this way you start from the abstract or general term "universe" and finally arrive at the concrete or specific address 1046 Allen Street, Santa Fe, New Mexico, United States, and so on.

Here is another sentence that illustrates an abstract statement:

A person walked down the street.

How can it be made more specific?

Abstract	Concrete
a person	Why keep the name a secret? Give a name: Janice Newland.
walked	What kind of walk? Make it better by describing the walk: "paced," "ambled," "strode," "sauntered," "strolled." (See where a good vocabulary can help?)
street	Name the street: Park Place.

Here are the two sentences together. Compare them.

1. A person walked down the street.
2. Janice Newland strode down Park Place.

Is there any doubt that the second sentence is more descriptive?

Try to improve your sentences by employing specific, concrete

EXERCISE 7

Write a paragraph in support of *one* of these topic sentences. Use an anecdote.

1. My neighbors like (dislike) little children.
2. Cheating can hurt more than it helps.
3. Mail service is worse than it was.
4. Trouble in the stands is not uncommon at sports events.
5. Children will not let anything interrupt their playing.

Tips on Including Specific Examples in Sentences

You will probably want to use as many examples as you can in your first few papers. (It's always easier to *cut down* on extra examples than to add them, so be generous.)

When you include examples, be sure to fit them into the flow of your paragraphs. Remember that you are writing a paragraph, not simply listing results or facts. Here are some specific suggestions about introducing examples:

1. Avoid the awkward phrase "An example of this is. . . ."
2. Don't overwork "for example" or "for instance." Use these expressions only once or twice in an essay, not more. You can include plenty of examples without pointing to them with "for instance."
3. Try putting "for example" in the *middle* of sentences: "The hook and ladder, for example, is over 20 years old."
4. When they begin a sentence, "for instance" and "for example" are followed by a comma. When they come in the middle of a sentence, they are *surrounded* by commas.
5. Make sure the words that follow "for example" and "for instance" make a complete sentence. Don't write: "For example, swimming in the river every summer." This is not a complete sentence. *Who* went swimming? "For example, we went swimming in the river every summer." This is a complete sentence.
6. The words "such as" can never begin a sentence.
7. Don't add a colon (:) after "for example" or "for instance" if either one introduces a complete sentence. (For the right way to use a colon, see page 182.)

Concrete Language

An important fact to realize about language is that it can be abstract (or general) on the one hand, and concrete (or specific) on the other.

FRANK W. MORRIS

DRE 006   4 FEB 80

words as often as possible. There will be some occasions when you will want to choose abstract terms, but for most writing, be as concrete as you can.

Abstract to Concrete

1. Replace vague words with precise ones:
   (a) We had something to eat.
   (b) The *four of us devoured* the *pancakes*.
2. Substitute names:
   (a) He liked his car.
   (b) *Harry* liked his new *Buick*.
3. Supply lively verbs:
   (a) The train passed the crossing.
   (b) The *express roared* past the crossing.
   (c) The *local rumbled* past the crossing.

Name names, give measurements, specify times, tell dates.

EXERCISE 8

FUNNY

Underline the specific (concrete) words in the following letter:*

Letter to a Landlady

By Judith Viorst

Dear Mrs. Schwaab:

I'm sure you're not expecting your beach house to look exactly the same as it did before you rented it to our family. (Ha! Ha!)

On the other hand, maybe you ought to read this note before you actually open the door.

We've located two of the five dresser drawers of your Early American dresser, and I hope the rest will turn up very soon. You might try digging around in the back of your yard, where my boys passed many a happy summer hour playing Buried Treasure.

Needless to say, we intend to replace the drapes. Little Lucy Porter (her folks spent a couple of days with us down here) was just beginning to master cutting with scissors, and she wasn't aware that curtains were a no—no.

Let me explain that telephone bill for the three long distance calls to Peking, China. We were drinking with the Cowans one night (they spent a couple of days with us down here), and I guess we decided it might be fun to call Mao.

*Copyright © 1972 by Judith Viorst.

In regard to your living room furniture. As you can see, I've already recovered the couch, and if you insist, I'll also have the chair done. The spaghetti sauce was on its way from the kitchen to the table, when Alexander swatted a fly and missed.

The indoor-outdoor carpet that you used to keep indoors might look better outdoors from now on. Under a tree—covered with a picnic table and some fallen leaves—it wouldn't be nearly as easy to see the spots.

A one-coat paint job (two at most) should certainly put your ceiling back in shape. Nobody in our family will acknowledge letting the bathtub overflow, so it must have been the Tuckers. (They spent a couple of days with us down here.)

Milton, you'll be pleased to see, has already patched the kicked-in parts on your screens. While that little Joey Kalb (the Kalbs spent a couple of days with us down here) is a beautiful child, he is also quite a kicker.

Sorry about that mattress on Nick's bed. Where he got the notion that he could use it as a raft, I'll never know.

I'm well aware that that Tiffany lamp was virtually irreplaceable, but we certainly plan to do the best we can. Opposed as I am to games of indoor baseball, what else is left when it rains for four days straight?

The new set of dishes almost matches the old ones, and I hope they will do. Lee and Lou Chandler (they spent a couple of days with us down here) offered to load the dishwasher Friday night, and sad to say they were much too loaded to load.

The cut on Anthony's head where he fell down the stairs is almost healed, but we couldn't get all the bloodstains off the wall. A 12-by-16 painting, however, hung at ankle level, should just about hide them.

Joan and Freddie Jackson (they spent a couple of days with us down here) will mail back the bedspread as soon as it's been rewoven. Their dog is a cute little rascal, but chews a lot.

It's really too bad about the full-length mirror, the good wine glasses, the windows in the guest room —and you'll also see that your vegetable garden was trampled. Helen and David Brunson (they spent a couple of days with us down here) decided to get di-

Par. III.	Tomatoes require frequent weeding and pruning.
Par. IV.	There are many interesting ways to cook tomatoes.
Par. V.	CONCLUSION

What topic in this outline is not related to the point in the thesis sentence? Are all the main body paragraphs about *raising* tomatoes? No. Paragraph IV is about *cooking* tomatoes; so it would be inappropriate for this particular essay.

Rule: Each main body paragraph must be about one particular aspect of the thesis sentence.

Example

Here is a rough outline of an essay on the topic of buying a used car.

Par. I.	INTRODUCTION
Thesis sentence	It pays to do some planning before buying a used car.
Par. II.	Decide which type of car best suits your needs.
Par. III.	Figure out how much you can afford to pay.
Par. IV.	Ask an expert mechanic for an opinion.
Par. V.	CONCLUSION

How does this compare to the preceding outline? Here are the questions to ask:

1. Does each idea for a paragraph represent a separate subject or main idea without overlapping other paragraphs? (In this case the answer is yes.)
2. Does each idea relate clearly to the point of the thesis sentence? (In this case the answer is yes.)

Since both answers are yes, this outline shows promise.

EXERCISE 16

Make up a rough outline for an essay by filling in the blank spaces. Make each of your entries a complete sentence. (Don't write a conclusion.)

1. *Topic:* What makes a good restaurant?

Par. I. Thesis sentence _____

_____

Par. II. _____

_____

Par. III.———————————————————

———————————————————

Par. IV.———————————————————

———————————————————

Par. V. CONCLUSION

2. *Topic:* Some people are entirely predictable.

Par. I. Thesis sentence———————————

———————————————————

Par. II.———————————————————

———————————————————

Par. III.———————————————————

———————————————————

Par. IV.———————————————————

———————————————————

Par. V. CONCLUSION

3. *Topic:* What's wrong with high schools?

Par. I. Thesis sentence———————————

———————————————————

Par. II.———————————————————

———————————————————

Par. III.———————————————————

———————————————————

Par. IV.———————————————————

———————————————————

Par. V. CONCLUSION

4. *Topic:* Prices keep rising.

Par. I. Thesis sentence: ———————————

———————————————————

Par. II.———————————————————

———————————————————

Par. III.———————————————————

———————————————————

Par. IV. _____

_____

Par. V. CONCLUSION

5. *Topic:* Needed: Better transportation.

Par. I. Thesis sentence _____

_____

Par. II. _____

_____

Par. III. _____

_____

Par. IV. _____

_____

Par. V. CONCLUSION

For paragraphs in an essay

Ask yourself:

1. Are all the paragraphs really about separate points?
2. Do all the points clearly relate to the thesis sentence?

ORDERING PARAGRAPHS WITHIN THE ESSAY

When you write an essay, you have total control over the order in which you will present your ideas. It's wise to plan the order in advance, when you are in the process of deciding which major points to make. Look at one example of an outline with good order:

Topic	How Students Can Choose a College
Par. I. Thesis sentence	Potential college students need information to help them decide on which school to attend.
Par. II. Topic sentence	*At first,* students can consult their high school guidance counselors.
Par. III. Topic sentence	*Next,* they can question friends and relatives who attend the college.
Par. IV. Topic sentence	*Last,* students can visit the campus to see what it is like.
Par. V.	Conclusion

Chronological Order

Those italicized words at the beginning of each topic sentence show that the order is related to time. The first step is listed first; the second, next; and the final step comes last. The words that begin the topic sentences tell the reader that the essay is switching from one idea to another. They are cues, like the indentation that begins each new paragraph. In this case the words "at first, "next," and "last" tell the reader that the points are being discussed in the order in which they would most likely happen. This is called *chronological order*, which means order related to *time*. Can you think of any other sets of three opening words that would also convey the idea of chronological order? List some:

_____   _____   _____

_____   _____   _____

_____   _____   _____

Order of Importance

There is another, equally valid order for the points in this essay. Ask yourself which of the three topic sentences appears to be the *most important*. Suppose it was paragraph III, questioning friends and relatives. Then the essay would be arranged in a different way:

Topic	How Students Can Choose a College.
Par. I. Thesis sentence	Potential students need information to help them decide on which college to attend.
Par. II. Topic sentence	*One important* thing students can do is consult their high school guidance counselors.
Par. III. Topic sentence	*Another* step is to make a personal visit to the campus.
Par. IV. Topic sentence	*Most important*, the student should ask friends and relatives who attend the college what it is really like.
Par. V.	Conclusion

Did you notice the change? The most important step comes at the end, and the opening words of paragraph IV make it clear that the last step is the most important one. This type of arrangement is called *order of importance*. In using it, put the vital point at the end, drawing attention to it with suitable opening words. Can you think of any other sets of opening words that convey the idea of order of importance? List them:

_____ _____ _____

_____ _____ _____

_____ _____ _____

Some ideas, then, can be arranged according to chronological order, and others can be listed in order of importance. As you have just seen, some topics can be ordered in _either_ way, depending on how you decide. The crucial point to remember is that ordering paragraphs within an essay makes your writing clearer and tighter. To reinforce the order, to make the essay even tighter, use words at the opening of your topic sentences to bind the ideas together.

EXERCISE 17

Which of the following sets can be used for order of importance? Which for chronological order? Which would work for both? (Mark them I, C, or Both.)

_____ 1. Par. II.   First, . . .
       Par. III. Second, . . .
       Par. IV.   Third, . . .

_____ 2. Par. II.   First, . . .
       Par. III. Furthermore, . . .
       Par. IV.   Last, . . .

_____ 3. Par. II.   At the outset, . . .
       Par. III. Afterwards, . . .
       Par. IV.   At the end, . . .

_____ 4. Par. II.   To begin with, . . .
       Par. III. Next, . . .
       Par. IV.   Finally, . . .

_____ 5. Par. II.   One thing . . .
       Par. III. Then, . . .
       Par. IV.   Most important . . .

EXERCISE 18

The main body ideas in the following outlines are in no particular order. Arrange each in either order of importance or chronological order, being careful to choose appropriate opening words. Be able to say which order you've chosen.

1. _Topic:_   Examinations are awful.
Thesis sentence   Examinations are not a good measure of learning because they put too much pressure on students.

Topic sentence	Most students get nervous in an exam room.
Topic sentence	Everyone stays up too late cramming.
Topic sentence	At the end of an exam, students rush their answers and make careless mistakes. Conclusion

_____

_____

_____

_____

_____

_____

2. *Topic:*	An Unpleasant Neighbor
Thesis sentence	Mr. Reynolds is the touchiest man on the block.
Topic sentence	He calls the police when someone is walking down the street after dark.
Topic sentence	He screams at children playing on the sidewalk on their way home from school.
Topic sentence	He orders his dog to attack anyone who steps on the lawn. Conclusion

_____

_____

_____

_____

_____

_____

3. *Topic*:	Decorating a Room
Thesis sentence	Decorating a living room in style takes real skill.
Topic sentence	A sense of shape and color is essential.

Topic sentence	Effectively mixing different periods and styles is difficult.
Topic sentence	Comfort and practicality should not be overlooked. Conclusion

_____

_____

_____

_____

_____

_____

_____

4. *Topic*:	Failing a Course
Thesis sentence	Sometimes it takes real dedication to flunk a course in this college.
Topic sentence	Not showing up for the final is a guaranteed method of failing.
Topic sentence	A student can cut classes in order to avoid learning anything from lectures or discussion.
Topic sentence	Cheating on assignments is a time-tested way of earning an F. Conclusion

_____

_____

_____

_____

_____

_____

_____

5. *Topic:*	Sunday Nights
Thesis sentence	Knowing that Monday brings another week of work always makes me depressed on Sunday nights.
Topic sentence	I put off going to bed until way after I should.

Topic
  sentence

Topic
  sentence

After dinner I just mope around
  the house.

The later it gets, the more I snap
  at my family.

_____

_____

_____

_____

_____

_____

_____

Introductions and Conclusions

THE INTRODUCTORY PARAGRAPH

The introductory paragraph presents the subject and states the thesis sentence or main point that you want your readers to recognize. First impressions count as much in writing as in shaking hands, so it is wise to take care that your introduction gets you and your essay off to a good start.

An introduction comes at the beginning of an essay, but first you should decide on the thesis sentence, the one sentence that contains the main point of the whole essay. Only when you have a satisfactory thesis sentence should you begin thinking about how to introduce the essay.

The reason for saving the introduction until after the thesis sentence is written should be obvious; you cannot introduce a point until you know what that point is.

It may help to think of a diagram that goes step by step:

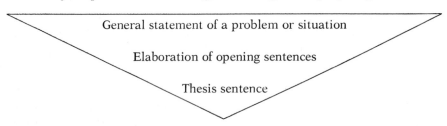

General statement of a problem or situation

Elaboration of opening sentences

Thesis sentence

A good introduction will lead up to the thesis sentence you have written first, and the thesis sentence will lead naturally into the discussion in the three main body paragraphs. However, the issue here is what you should do to find the best way of leading up to that thesis sentence.

Look at a good introduction from a paper on the topic of crime in our cities.

> Every year the FBI issues statistics on the rate of violent crime, and every year there is an increase, particularly in our cities. Politicians, judges, lawyers, and plain citizens are becoming more and more aware that we have been too easy on the criminals who are making our cities dangerous places to live in. It is time we realized that urban crime can be stopped by giving longer jail sentences to convicted criminals.

Questions

1. How has the topic been narrowed down to the thesis sentence?
2. Does the narrowing happen all at once or is it gradual?
3. How does the writer move from "crime" in the first sentence to "longer jail sentences" in the thesis sentence?
4. What will the three main body paragraphs say?

There are five ways to begin solid, informative introductions that make your reader want to read further:

1. Ask a question.   The rest of the introduction, and the thesis sentence in particular, will provide the answer.

Example

Topic: Self-Knowledge
Did you ever stop to think what you were doing one year ago? Most people don't. Wrapped up in the present or busy looking toward the future, they don't take much interest in the past. But if you do ask yourself about the recent past, you can discover who you really are and what is important to you.

2. State an alarming fact, problem, or statistic.   (The preceding sample introduction about crime does this.) The rest of the introduction will lead up to the suggestion in the thesis sentence, and the rest of the essay will show how the problem can be solved.

3. Define an important word.   The introduction will also define the "key" word that signals the particular point you want to make in your essay.

Example

Topic: Marriage
The dictionary defines marriage as a legally recognized, close, and intimate union of a man and a woman. The two people in love who decide to get married are entering into a legal contract set up by society. What are the legal implications of two people getting married? What are their obligations

as defined by the society around them? Lawyers and judges have offered very different opinions on the subject.

(Notice how this paper wisely avoids tackling the whole vague question of marriage by narrowing the subject down to the *legal* implications. Another paper could have done the same kind of narrowing by dealing only with love, or children, or fidelity, or shared goals. Any five-paragraph essay that tried to handle *all* the meanings of marriage would be hopelessly vague.)

4. Start with a quotation.   Elaborate on it for your thesis sentence.

Example

Topic: Marriage
There is an old saying that "marriages are made in heaven." It may be more true than we think. People decide to spend their lives together for many different reasons. But the marriages that last are the ones based on a strong spiritual bond.

5. Disagree with accepted wisdom.   State what most people think and then, in the thesis sentence, say what *you* think. The rest of the essay will go on to support your point.

Example

Topic: Hard Work
Most people believe that if you work hard, you will be rewarded. There is a whole set of proverbs to back up this belief, and little children are always told the benefits of perseverence. But all around us we can see examples of how hard work simply does not pay off, and how some people who do no work at all seem to get richer and richer.

There are three strategies to avoid in introductions:

1. Never give an outline.   The readers will get into the main body of the essay soon enough. In the introduction you want to get them into the mood to agree with your points, so lead them into the essay slowly.

Example to Avoid

In my essay I will talk about. . . .
I will tell you the three things you need to know in order to. . . .

2. Never announce that you don't know much about the topic.   When you don't know much about a topic, you have two choices: pick another one, or find out about the one you chose. Never say that you don't know or don't care. (But, when you deal with a difficult or speculative topic that nobody knows much about, by all means say that you are only offering a suggestion or a possibility.)

Example to Avoid

I never really understood all the fuss about pollution, but here's what I think. . . .

3. Never be too general.   Remember that you are moving from the general (opening) to the less general (middle) to the specific (thesis sentence). Make sure your middle sentences are more specific than the opening ones. Aim them toward the thesis.

Example to Avoid

Topic: Dangers in the Environment
   In the past few years Americans have become aware that towns with certain industries have higher cancer rates than the national average. This is a problem.

(Do you see how "This is a problem" does not get more specific, and how it does not lead toward a thesis?)
   Here is the same introduction rewritten, with a good, narrow middle sentence.

   In the past few years Americans have become aware that towns with certain industries have higher cancer rates than the national average. In southern and eastern New Jersey, where there is a high concentration of chemical plants, cancer rates are very high. The same is true for sections of the Gulf Coast, where cancer rates seem to increase when certain industries are located in groups. It is now believed that many forms of cancer result from industrial pollution.

EXERCISE 19

Begin the following introductory paragraphs with a sentence or two of your own.

1. *Topic:* Competitive Sports

_____

_____

_____

In addition, competitive sports are capable of developing a winning attitude in the people who play them. But to me, the most important benefit from competitive sports is the exercise they provide.

2. *Topic:* The College Library

_____

_____

_____

They come there to get away from the noise of the student center or the hubbub of the campus lounge. But many of the students who search for peace and quiet will be disappointed. Thanks to a few inconsiderate students, the library is the noisiest place on the whole campus.

3. *Topic:* Comparison Shopping

_____

_____

_____

A good part of this money is spent foolishly on expensive things that could have been bought for far less. People could save hundreds of dollars if they would take the trouble to compare prices before they buy large items like cars, washing machines, and television sets.

4. *Topic:* Today's Newspaper

_____

_____

_____

In it will be a whole series of features that have little or nothing to do with the major news stories of the day. Besides supplying news, the daily paper is a means of providing service, advice, and entertainment for the whole family.

5. *Topic:* Pets

_____

_____

_____

Whatever it is, it helps to identify the type of person you are. Like your clothing, your car, and your furniture, the pet you own reveals important parts of your personality.

EXERCISE 20

Write five introductory paragraphs, using the topics and thesis sentences presented in Exercise 18. Try to vary the introductory techniques you use.

THE CONCLUDING PARAGRAPH

Essays do not simply end suddenly. A separate, brief paragraph ties together everything that has been said about the thesis sentence. This final paragraph answers the question "so what?" It wraps up the entire essay and gives the reader the feeling that the essay has reached a real goal.

There are two different points to remember about writing conclusions. First you must show your readers that you have finished what you set out to say. The introductory paragraph gave the thesis sentence, the main point of the essay. The concluding paragraph shows that your train of thought begun with the thesis sentence is ended.

Second, your conclusion should be clearly related to the main body paragraphs. It is not a catchall for leftover evidence or examples that should have been in earlier paragraphs. Neither is a conclusion the place to begin a new, unrelated train of thought.

Remember that your readers will get their final impression of your thinking from the conclusion. What they will take away depends in large part upon the way you end the essay. A poor conclusion can weaken a good essay, while an especially forceful conclusion can make a weak essay sound a bit stronger.

Good Conclusions

Good conclusions work in different ways:

1.   **They answer the question "So what?"**   They drive home the points made earlier.

Example

Sports, then, are an immense program of popular entertainment. The different teams and games serve to take everyday concerns off people's minds by diverting them with action, drama, and heroism. This "safety valve" function might be the most important role sports can play; they give Americans a chance to escape from reality.

2.   **They emphasize the important points.**   Points mentioned in the main body paragraphs are restated briefly and directly.

Example

Violence cannot be separated from sports. The most violent sports—boxing, football, hockey, auto racing—are among the most popular. It all adds up to a single point: Violence is an essential part of the sports we all watch.

3.   **They raise an important question and answer it.**   (Where do we go from here?)

Example

Are sports the key to understanding Americans? I think they are. As a national form of escape, they show where our true values lie.

4.   **They may employ a quotation.**   Words said by well-known people help to sum up the point of the thesis sentence.

Example

"Winning is the only thing" was the motto of a great coach, Vince Lombardi. If athletes believed this saying, sports would be much more violent than they are. The stress on winning is far too important among our coaches and adults today, and can have harmful effects on all young children.

5. **They can show the need for a change in attitude or behavior.**

Example

Merely watching sports can drug the mind. Playing them, on the other hand, invigorates the mind. An active participant will not only get good exercise, but will also experience honest competition and good sportsmanship. Instead of just spending time as observers, people ought to be out there playing and participating.

Each one of the preceding five conclusions has concluded the writer's train of thought decisively and to the point.

Bad Conclusions

On the other hand, there are certain tendencies to avoid in concluding paragraphs.

1. **Never simply repeat your thesis or say "as you just saw" or "as I just told you."** A five-paragraph essay is not so long that a reader will forget what went before.

Example to Avoid

As I have told you in my previous paragraphs, sports are an essential part of America's way of life.

2. **Never give a bare summary.** You may sometimes restate previous points in different form, but a conclusion can never repeat all the points one by one.

Example to Avoid

So, in summary, let me repeat my points. First . . .

3. **Avoid phrases like "in conclusion."** Such phrases have been worn out from years of overuse. (The other common phrase to avoid is "Last but not least . . . ")

Example to Avoid

In conclusion, I would like to say that the way people play sports says much about the way they think of themselves.

4. **Never say that you are not sure of yourself.** If you don't know much about a particular topic, pick something else. (This does not mean, of course, that you have to act as if you know everything about the subject.)

Example to Avoid

Though I don't know much about sports, it seems to me that the examples I have given demonstrate that they do show America's best side to the world.

5.   **Never give orders or deliver a sermon.**   Your point may be truly inspired, but remember that you must convince your readers. They will not believe you just because you punctuate with an exclamation mark, or because you underline a word or two. (There are legitimate ways to employ a strong call for action; see number 5 in the preceding discussion on "Good Conclusions.")

Example to Avoid

So get out and participate. Don't just sit there and watch! Sports are for *everyone*. Nobody is too old or too young. Get out and play *some* sport.

6.   **Avoid overstatement.**   A five-paragraph essay is not likely to give the final word on the subject. Do not make extravagant claims.

Example to Avoid

Sports are, therefore, the most wonderful thing that could possibly take place. If everyone would take part in some form of sport, the world would be a perfect place.

7.   **Never make points that have no connection with the thesis sentence.**   You cannot hope to begin a whole new train of thought in a conclusion.

Example to Avoid

Sports are only one of the ways we can see the true character of America. I could have shown the same thing from a look at dating habits or from the way we run our political campaigns.

EXERCISE 21

In Exercise 18 of the preceding section, "The Essay," are five different rough outlines for a work assignment. Using the same thesis sentences and topic sentences, write a conclusion for each one. Be able to say which conclusion technique (1 through 5 of "Good Conclusions") you are following.

EXERCISE 22

Write an essay with *two separate conclusions*. Pick any two techniques listed at the beginning of this section. At the end of the essay, label your separate conclusions A and B. The idea is to write each conclusion as if it were the only possible one for your essay, in order to get an idea of the choices available to you.

Write your essay on one of these topics:

1. Some people never learn from experience.
2. Love and marriage do not always go together.
3. Natural foods are becoming more popular.
4. Knowing facts is not real understanding.
5. A taste for _____ music can make life more enjoyable. (Choose any type of music you wish.)
6. Little children ought to have playmates from all different backgrounds.
7. Sex education is valuable.
8. A big city offers all kinds of opportunities.
9. Actions speak louder than words.
10. Some teenagers never consider their parents' problems.

EXERCISE 23

Go back to the beginning of this section and look at the five good concluding paragraphs. In the space below, write in an appropriate thesis sentence for each. You will have to make some guesses, of course, but see if you can figure out how these essays were *introduced*:

Conclusion 1

Thesis sentence: _____

_____

Conclusion 2

Thesis sentence: _____

_____

Conclusion 3

Thesis sentence: _____

_____

Conclusion 4

Thesis sentence: _____

_____

Conclusion 5

Thesis sentence: _____

_____

CHAPTER 2

TYPES OF WRITING

Description

Most writing involves description. The two types of description you will find most useful are

1. Description of a place
2. Description of a person

DESCRIPTION OF A PLACE

For descriptive paragraphs and short essays it is best to limit the description to a small place—a room, a house—instead of something as large as a city or a country. You want to create such a vivid impression of the place that you make the reader see what you see. In order to *show* the reader the place, you must provide vivid, concrete details.

There are two ways to go about writing a description of a place. Start from the overall impression and break it down into the details, or start from the details and build up toward an overall impression. Let's look at these one at a time, first considering the general-to-specific description.

General Impression to Details

Take a place you know well, like your room at home. What is your general feeling about it? What sentence can describe it? When you have that sentence, you have a topic sentence for a paragraph or even a thesis sentence for a whole essay. Then you need to back up that sentence with specifics. What details prove your point? What will support your general impression?

When you write such a descriptive paragraph, remember that the topic sentence has to be narrow and specific, too. You can't say "My room is a nice place" and expect your readers to be interested. Instead you have to supply a much more specific kind of topic sentence that offers a value judgement:

My room at home is the messiest part of the house.

or

My room is the only place in the world where I can be alone.

or

I have decorated my room with cast-off furniture I found in the basement.

These sentences are good because they will lead to tight, unified paragraphs. Compared to "I like my room" or "My room is comfortable," they are much more successful in drawing the reader's interest.

When you have pinpointed a specific impression of the room in your topic sentence, expand on it by supplying descriptive details that will back it up. Here is an example:

My room at home is the messiest part of the house. I am not usually considered a slob by my friends, but that's only because they have never seen how I live. My room is too small for all the junk I collect, so it is scattered about the floor, hung on the walls, and draped on the furniture. On the floor is my magazine collection, with some issues dating back to the early 1960s. Under the bed are boxes from old Christmas presents. The closets won't close because they are crammed full with luggage, old childhood toys, clothing for winter and summer, and my rock collection. On the wall, gathering dust, are pictures I clipped from fan magazines when I was in junior high. I never got around to taking them down because my record collection gets in the way and I'd have to move that first before I could reach them.

EXERCISE 1

Write 5 one-paragraph impressions of different places. Start with an impression, narrow it down, and provide three concrete sense details to back it up. Use these places:

1. A classroom

Impression: _____

Detail 1. _____

Detail 2. _____

Detail 3. _____

2. An auditorium, theater, or movie house

Impression: _____

Detail 1. _____

Detail 2. _____

Detail 3. _____

3. A coffee shop

Impression: _____

Detail 1. _____

Detail 2. _____

Detail 3. _____

4. A store

Impression: _____

Detail 1. _____

Detail 2. _____

Detail 3. _____

5. A library

Impression: _____

Detail 1. _____

Detail 2. _____

Detail 3. _____

From Details to Overall Impression

Another, equally good method of developing a description is by listing the specific *sense* (smell, touch, and so on) details first and then grouping them together into categories. Let's take the cafeteria at college as an example. Look at this list of all the concrete, vivid details one student identified.

1. Greasy hamburgers piled on the steam table
2. Watery coffee in a styrofoam cup
3. Bored students playing endless games of bridge
4. Rock music on the speaker system

5. Bits of napkins and plastic plates scattered on the floor
6. Huge piles of refuse heaped around the litter bins
7. Salt and pepper in little paper envelopes
8. Ashtrays overflowing with cigarette butts
9. People late for class who sneak into line
10. Stale apple pie on a cardboard tray
11. Tables shoved close together
12. Antiseptic green walls without pictures
13. Students yelling across the room at friends
14. Two bored cashiers talking about soap operas
15. Half the tables empty by two o'clock

These are good details; they show that the student really looked at that cafeteria carefully. Now they have to be grouped into categories because the list above doesn't have any order to it.

Can you think of any categories suggested by the list? How about:

A. The food
B. The atmosphere
C. The people

These three categories would include almost every item on the list and at the same time organize the three main-body paragraphs of a five-paragraph essay.

EXERCISE 2

Organize the list into the three categories:

A. Food _____

_____

_____

_____

_____

B. Atmosphere _____

_____

_____

_____

_____

C. People _____

_____

_____

_____

_____

Now that the details are in categories, can you come up with a statement, in sentence form, that characterizes each grouping? The sentence will be your topic sentence, so it cannot be too vague or broad. It must express the characteristics you have already identified by means of the list of details, as in this example of a topic sentence for category one, the food:

    The food at our cafeteria is terrible.

or

    If you want decent food, don't bother with our cafeteria.

or

    Our cafeteria's food is about three steps below McDonald's.

Your details have led you to this statement, and you have already backed it up by your observations. You are now ready to write the paragraph on the food, making use of each detail on the list that relates to the food.

EXERCISE 3

Write three possible topic sentences for each of the other two categories, atmosphere and people.

Atmosphere: Three topic sentences

Sentence 1._____

_____

Sentence 2._____

_____

Sentence 3._____

_____

People: Three topic sentences

Sentence 1._____

_____

Sentence 2._____

_____

Sentence 3._____

_____

When you have written topic sentences for the three main-body paragraphs, you are ready to form the thesis sentence, the one sentence that will give the main point of the entire essay. To get this sentence, look at the various details and the three topic sentences you have. What overall idea do they convey? What attitude toward the cafeteria do they suggest? Take that idea or attitude, put it into a sentence, and you have your thesis.

A thesis sentence, three topic sentences, and good details should give you enough raw material to construct a good essay. If you've arrived at it in what seems like a backward approach (and it is certainly the reverse of the procedure followed in Chapter 1 and the first part of this chapter), there is a good reason for it. This way of building a descriptive essay, starting from sharp details and working toward more general statements about them, is successful in writing description.

EXERCISE 4

List fifteen sharp, concrete, specific *sense* (sight, sound, smell, touch, taste) details about *one* of the following places:
1. A park
2. A room in a public building
3. A street
4. A backyard
5. A playground
6. A gymnasium
7. A vacant field
8. A busy street intersection
9. An office
10. A restaurant

Go and look at the place. Listen to the noises. Pick out the sense impressions you get. Sniff, touch, use all your senses.

EXERCISE 5

Organize the details from Exercise 4 into three groups. Write a topic sentence that will introduce each different group. (If some of your details don't fit in, leave them out.) Then write one thesis sentence that will cover all three topic sentences and every group of details. Finally, write an essay, using your three topic sentences and the thesis sentence that applies to them. Include an introduction and a conclusion.

DESCRIPTION OF A PERSON

People can be described in the same manner as places; you may choose inpressions first and then come up with details, or you may start with details and work toward an overall impression. But the most important fact to keep in mind is the need to relate your details to the person's character. You want to describe what makes this person tick, so every detail you include has to work toward illustrating some side of the personality. Does she love music? What detail will show it best? Does his personality change from day to day? Hour to hour? Illustrate the change by describing specific behavior.

In a description of a person you must be selective. You cannot write a biography or tell everything you know; that would take far too long. Instead you must work toward creating a single, dominant impression. This impression, a kind of thumbnail sketch, will become the main idea of the description. Choose details to support this impression, and leave out any detail that is too general.

Finally, you should try to describe the dominant impression gradually. There is no need to tell as much as you can all at once. Readers need to be shown characteristics slowly; it gives them a chance to find out about the person as they would do if they were to meet him face to face. After all, no one learns everything about another person at a first meeting, and even first impressions may change in time.

Example (A one-paragraph description of a person)*

The master of River Valley Farm, Herbert William Clutter, was forty-eight years old, and as a result of a recent medical examination for an insurance policy, knew himself to be in first-rate condition. Though he wore rimless glasses and was of but average height, standing just under five feet ten, Mr. Clutter cut a man's-man figure. His shoulders were broad, his hair held its dark color, his square-jawed, confident face retained a healthy-hued youthfulness, and his teeth, unstained and strong enough to shatter walnuts, were still intact. He weighed a hundred and fifty-four—the same as he had the day he graduated from Kansas State University, where he had majored in agriculture. He was not as rich as the richest citizen in Holcomb—Mr. Taylor Jones, a neighboring rancher. He was, however, prominent both there and in Garden City, the close-by county seat, where he had headed the building committee for the newly completed First Methodist Church, an eight-hundred-thousand-dollar edifice. He was currently chairman of the Kansas Conference of Farm Organizations, and his name was everywhere respectfully recognized among Midwestern agriculturalists, as it was in certain Washington offices, where he had been a member of the Federal Farm Credit Board during the Eisenhower administration.

Comment This descriptive paragraph concentrates on the outside, the "public" side of its subject. There is no explanation of how the man

*From Truman Capote, *In Cold Blood* (New York: Random House 1965), p. 6.

felt or what he thought; rather, there is a kind of first impression based on his looks and the positions he held.

EXERCISE 6

Write three different descriptive paragraphs about someone you know well. Work from this list of the person's characteristics:

Physical characteristics
    Height
    Weight
    Build
    Coloring
    Hair (color and style)
    Eyes
    Ethnic background
    Speech

Social characteristics
    Family situation
    Friends
    Occupation
    Hobbies
    Education
    Place of birth

Personality and character
    Sense of humor
    Friendliness
    Goals in life
    Strengths
    Weaknesses

After you have compiled a list, write the three descriptive paragraphs. Make them as complete as possible, and order them in any way you like: physical, personality, or social, whichever strikes an observer first.

Process

An essay about a process has to explain and describe. The writer is the expert and the readers are the laymen. The writer's job is to make sure the readers understand every single step of the process as they are clearly guided through the whole operation.

It is hard to write about a process without knowing enough about the subject, but you will usually be describing something you know very well, something you yourself have studied or done. Even if you know your subject, the difficulty is in making the process crystal clear to your readers. Keep in mind that they may not have studied or performed the process themselves and are relying on you for instruction.

When thinking about readers, it's probably best to consider two separate functions of process essays. The first one explains and the second one describes how to do it.

Explains	Describes How to Do
The rules of chess	How to win at chess
How a car works	How to make a car run better
How heart attacks occur	How to avoid heart attacks

You can see from these examples that the first type of process essay is an explanation; the second is a description, a "how to do" essay. In the second, your readers actually want to *do* the process you write about, while in the first it may be quite impossible to do it yourself (how salmon return upstream to spawn; how gravity acts on objects).

Both types of process essays—the explanation and the "how to do"—are common. Many examinations in school call for an explanation (how the Ice Age began; how an embryo is formed); many descriptions to friends often call for "how to do" (how to get to Rochester; the best way to plant a terrarium). This section will concentrate on the "how to do" essay, the type you're probably most familiar with. At the end, special suggestions for the other type of process, the explanation, will be given.

PLANNING THE "HOW TO" ESSAY

The best way to describe "how to do" a process is to break it down into steps. Visualize the first step, then the next, and so on. . . .

Process: Changing a Tire

1. Move car to side of road, well away from traffic
2. Engage emergency brake
3. Remove spare tire from trunk
4. Take out jack and lug wrench
5. Take off hubcap
6. Start loosening tire nuts *before* the car is jacked up
7. When nuts are slightly loose, place the jack securely on the ground
8. Make sure jack contacts the car's underbody or frame
9. Put wood block under front (or back) tire to keep car from rolling off jack
10. Raise car only enough off ground so spare will fit on wheel
11. Remove nuts and tire
12. Put spare tire on
13. Tighten nuts on the spare loosely, not all the way

14. Lower car
15. Tighten nuts firmly, criss-crossing order of tightening
16. Replace hubcap; put jack, wrench, and tire in trunk
17. Check tire pressure; have tire fixed at a service station as soon as possible.

Those steps are going to be described in greater detail in the body of the essay, but at the planning stage it's important to know what steps you'll be describing later on.

After listing the steps, group them into categories. Which steps go together? For this topic, you can group them like this:

While car is still on the ground (steps 1 through 8)
Replacing flat with a spare (steps 9 through 13)
After spare is in place (steps 14 through 17)

All that is left is to write a brief introduction, perhaps reassuring your reader how easy or straightforward the process is; one or two sentences should be enough.

EXERCISE 7

Pick one of the following "how to do" processes and list all the separate steps. Then group the steps together into three or four main categories.

Processes: How to build a bookcase
How to buy a car
How to cook a steak
How to paint a room
How to find a job

Topic _____

Steps

1. _____

2. _____

3. _____

4. _____

5. _____

6. _____

7. _____

8. _____

9. _____

10. _____

Category A _____	Steps _____	to _____
Category B _____	Steps _____	to _____
Category C _____	Steps _____	to _____
Category D _____	Steps _____	to _____

Your essay will have as many main-body paragraphs as there are categories of steps. Some will have only three main-body paragraphs; some may have four or even more. The more complex the process, the more steps and categories of steps you will need. The main requirement is that you make every step clear to the reader.

ORDERING A "HOW TO" PAPER

The order of performing the process is strictly chronological; every step must follow the previous one. If one of the steps might possibly seem out of order, be clear about its proper place: "Take the crosspieces you have glued and set them aside to dry. While they are drying you can begin to work on the shelf supports." Or, "During the hottest part of the summer, water plants every day; you can cultivate before you water or after, depending on your preference."

If any step of the process could be confusing, be extra careful to clarify it immediately. Take the time to define all technical terms or unusual vocabulary. Don't use different names for the same thing. Think of your readers as having to do the process with your essay right in front of them. Because you won't be there to offer advice, your words on the page must tell the whole story. This advice applies to everything you write, of course, but in a process paper it is very important because one false or misleading step could ruin the whole essay, leaving your readers confused.

Example*
This selection of a "how to" process paper, taken from a sporting equipment catalogue, tells how hikers ought to take care of their feet while on the trail.

Care of Feet
Keep your toenails short. Socks should be changed at least twice a day, if possible, and if wet, immediately. Experienced climbers often stop by a brook or spring to wash their feet, rest them, and change socks. The socks can be tied on the outside of the pack to dry. When you wash your feet, do it quickly so as not to soften the skin, which tends to make it blister more easily.

Blisters should never be regarded lightly. They can lead to the type of infection that can only be cured by antibiotics. Keep the feet as clean as possible at all times. Medicated foot powder is a good idea, especially in the mountains. Simple talcum powder will work nearly as well. This is an inex-

*Copyright © Eastern Mountain Sports, Inc., September 1976.

pensive and effective insurance, helping to avoid athlete's foot and to keep the feet dry.

The best cure for blisters is prevention. Wearing a liner sock underneath heavy socks reduces friction between the boot and the foot and allows the bulk of the slippage to occur between the socks. Feeling for "hot spots" on your foot or ankle is the only way to check a blister before it occurs. If you feel a certain area is warm, chafed, and slightly red, take the time to put on some "Molefoam" or "Moleskin," available at any drugstore. Generously cut a section to cover the area well. Leave the Molefoam on until the hike is over. Experienced hikers always carry Moleskin or foam with them. If you don't need it, someone else might. Should you notice a "hot spot," and you're without Moleskin, use adhesive tape. Tape works better than Bandaids because it stays in place through rough treatment and friction and covers a larger area.

If a blister does develop, you may find it necessary to drain it in order to relieve the pressure and pain. First, sterilize a needle or the point of a knife in a match flame. After applying antiseptic to the area of the blister, carefully puncture it on the edge, not the top, and squeeze all the fluid out. Immediately apply more antiseptic and cover with a bandage or sterile gauze. If no more hiking is to be done, this should be adequate, but if you must continue to walk, place a piece of Moleskin or foam over the whole thing, bandage and all, to prevent further irritation.

Comment The entire passage is "how to do" advice; there is no introduction, since it comes from the middle of a page of outdoors information. The last paragraph describes one single process very clearly—how to treat a blister. Notice how the author carefully pointed out where to puncture the blister. The reader had a chance to go wrong here, but the author saw the difficulty and made the advice especially clear by writing "on the edge, not the top."

EXERCISE 8

Take a process from the list below and write a "how to do" essay about it. Assume that the reader has never done it before and wants very much to learn how.

How to learn to drive	How to make spaghetti
How to learn to swim	How to keep fit
How to study for an exam	How to decorate a room
How to take a test	How to light a campfire

EXERCISE 9

Use the "how to do" style in a different, perhaps humorous, way, on one of these topics:

How to fail a course	How to mess up a room
How to fall in love	How to have a bad vacation
How not to study	How to annoy a friend

EXPLANATION

When you explain how something happens, as opposed to describing how to do something, you must take a slightly different approach. Since you do not expect your readers to *do* the process, your job is to make them interested in what you have to explain. To get and keep their attention, you must demonstrate that you know what you are talking about and explain every point clearly. You may also pause over particularly interesting details. This doesn't break your chronological order, and it does give special emphasis and focus to your essay.

Example*

How a Dinner Is Served in the Sudan

The concern and respect shown to one's guest throughout Africa, and from which we can learn much, is no greater than in the Sudan. As a guest enters a Sudanese home, he is immediately offered *Abre* or *Tabrihana*, a refreshing non-alcoholic fruit drink only slightly sweetened so as not to dull the appetite. This is a symbolic gesture welcoming him after his "long journey."

Dinner is served on a low table. Guests are made comfortable on pillows decorated with ostrich feathers. The table is bare.

The Arabic custom of pouring water over the hands of the guests from the *Ebrig*, a handsome copper ewer [pitcher], and catching the water into an equally handsome copper basin is an important ritual in the Sudan. Each guest is offered a towel with which to wipe his hands. Large cloths to cover the knees are given to each guest in place of napkins.

Upon the signal of the host, dinner is served. It starts with soup, brought out in individual bowls on a huge, round, decorated copper tray. The large tray is placed on the table. Spoons are offered to the guests.

After the soup has been enjoyed, the entire tray is removed and a second larger tray is brought with all the dishes of the main course resting on beaded doilies made by the women. There may be five or six dishes to dip into. (No knives or forks are used, but spoons may be provided.) But most of the Sudanese eat the main course from common dishes using *Kisra* or *Khupz* (their great flat breads) to sop up the mixtures. Four dishes are individually served: the soup, the salad, the *Shata* (red-hot spice) and the dessert.

When the entree is served, small plates or bowls are also brought in from which the host or hostess dishes out portions of salad and gives each guest a spoon with which to eat the salad. Again hands are washed and everyone looks forward to dessert. Sweets like *Creme Caramela* are usually served and are preferred to fruits. No beverage is served with dinner, but one may ask for water. After dinner everyone relaxes and enjoys the famous *Guwah*, coffee served from the *Jebena*, the stunning little coffeepot from which it is poured into tiny cups. If tea is preferred, the succulent spiced teas with cloves or cinnamon are served. Finally an incense burner filled with sandalwood is placed in the center of the room, a touch leaving the guests with a feeling of delightful relaxation.

Comment   The whole process is broken down into easily followed

*From Bea Sandler, *The African Cookbook* (New York: T. Y. Crowell Company, 1970), pp. 16-17.

steps. All technical terms are explained briefly, so the reader can under-stand every item and process.

EXERCISE 10

Pick an operation or process you know about and describe it. It may be that you have job experience. If so, you could write "How a _____ (supermarket, clothing store, and so on) works." In such an essay you would describe deliveries, stockrooms, pricing policies and procedures (markups), selling strategies, security, and treatment of employees.

An alternative would be to describe and explain a process you have learned about in school or through a hobby. Some examples would be:

> How an engineer is trained
> How birds migrate
> How a bill becomes a law
> How a car's engine operates

Or, you may take a topic closer to home, one that describes a family or ethnic custom:

> How my family celebrates _____
> An Italian (Polish, Irish, and so on) wedding
> How my ancestors arrived in _____

You may want to employ the special technique of lingering over a particularly interesting step of the process to give your paper added focus and emphasis.

Definition

Definition crops up often in writing. Whenever you are dealing with unfamiliar technical terms, you may have to define them. Or, some of your ideas may not be clear to the average reader and so need clarifica-tion. Or there may come a time when you want to give a strictly per-sonal meaning to a common term, to put an ordinary word in a new light. These situations all call for definitions. The ability to get across a clear definition is a basic tool for anyone who writes.

There are different types of definitions: some may take only a line or even a word; some may take a paragraph; and some may require a whole essay. Let's look at the different categories, starting with the smallest and working up to a complex definition that would require a full five-paragraph essay.

BRIEF DEFINITION FOR CLARITY

Suppose you were writing about why you enjoyed rock music. In one of your paragraphs you might say:

> My favorite kind of rock has to be played at full volume on the stereo. With the sound turned all the way up, the drums and organ seem like they're right in the room, especially if the set's woofers are powerful.

Someone who knew about stereo sets would know that the word "woofer" refers to the part of the speaker that handles the low notes. Would every reader know it? That is a decision you have to make. If you suspect that many readers would not know what "woofer" meant, a brief definition would clarify the term. Your sentence would read:

> With the sound turned all the way up, the drums and organ seem like they're right in the room, especially if the set's woofers, the speakers that handle the low notes, are powerful.

This is a brief definition for clarity, an attempt to make sure that your readers understand a term that may be unfamiliar.

When you are writing for people you know well, you hardly ever have doubts over whether to define a term. If you were to write that essay about rock music for an audience of musicians, you would not have to define "woofer." If you were sure that your readers were not musicians or owners of stereos, you *would* have to define "woofer." The difficult decisions come when several groups compose your audience or when you don't know your audience very well. There is no exact rule to apply in such situations, but it is usually better to supply a brief definition when in doubt. Below are three common ways of supplying brief definitions:

1. *Give a synonym, a word that means the same.*
     We all sat down to a meal of coke, french fries, and grinders, sometimes called heroes or submarines.
2. *Give a very short definition right after the word.*
     She found the town in the gazetteer, the part of an atlas that lists place names.
     Every paper needs a bibliography, a list of the books on the subject.
3. *Rework the sentence so that it explains the unfamiliar term.*
     He finally put all his ideas together to make a synthesis.
     His gait was wrong; there was something disconnected about the way he shifted his arms and legs when he walked down the street.

EXERCISE 11

Write a sentence for each of the following words, including a brief definition of the word, as in the examples above:

1. nucleus	4. haughty
2. naive	5. catalyst
3. opportune	6. worsted

THE DEFINITION PARAGRAPH

One of the best ways of explaining a very general term or an abstract idea is to define it briefly and then expand the definition by giving specific examples that illustrate it. The specific examples make the definition concrete, and therefore easier to understand. Notice how this is done in the following example.

Example

"Prejudice" means making up one's mind before looking at the facts. All little children have prejudices about food; they don't want to eat spinach because they don't think they'll like it, even though they have never eaten it before. Adults share this kind of irrational judgment. How many people will say they don't like modern art or Japanese food without ever having had a chance to find out what they are like? The same holds true for the more vicious forms of prejudice, which are usually directed at ethnic groups on the basis of little or no solid knowledge. In this sense, prejudice is more than an irrational dislike; it is a positively harmful and potentially dangerous attitude.

The writer of this paragraph moved from a common kind of prejudice that children and adults display to a different, dangerous kind that has elements of hostility in it. It's a good definition, for it supports the topic sentence with specific examples.

EXERCISE 12

Take a term that you have a personal meaning for. Write *two* definition paragraphs, one defining what *most people* think and one giving *your own* definition. Here are some words you might choose to define.

home	friendship
style	cop-out
honesty	cheap
patriotism	old-fashioned
expensive	intelligence
vacation	dramatic
silly	sensitive
personality	common sense

Before you make your choice you may find it helpful to check the dictionary for the most common uses of the word you pick. Your personal meaning will not be the same as the dictionary's meaning. If it is, pick another word.

THE DEFINITION ESSAY

This essay, often called an extended definition, is very much like a definition paragraph in that it is also best developed through the use of examples. It is usually much more personal, though. The definition is not so much what the dictionary says, but more like "What the word means to me."

If you were to look up the word "love" in the dictionary, you would find all the commonly accepted meanings. But you would not find exactly what that word meant to you, nor *what you think it should mean* to people. In other words, you cannot find a personal meaning in a dictionary; that definition must come from you.

If you were to look up the word "friendship," you would find that the dictionary gives *every* meaning in common use, but not the very particular meaning it has for you. In your essay you would have to narrow down that dictionary definition to the precise significance you place on the word. You would have to write of examples you know of friendship, of specific situations that clearly show your readers what the word means to you. Do you know of an instance when someone you know displayed true friendship? Then tell it to your reader. Do you know what the word does *not* mean to you? Then say so. You want to supply the meanings that matter most to you, not the general, abstract meaning given in the dictionary.

One good way of beginning a definition essay is to say what the word *does not* mean to you, or to say what the word means to other people. Then devote the rest of the essay to the contrast between that meaning and your own personal view. If you are writing a five-paragraph essay, you will have three separate aspects of the word, or three different ways of explaining its meaning. Let's take "friendship" and see how the definition can be arranged in the following exercise.

EXERCISE 13

Three meanings for friendship
1. Feeling of common goals in life
2. Willingness to help
3. No need for a false front

These may be the ones you want; now make them into topic sentences, and supply examples and details in the remaining paragraphs, and write the essay.

Three examples of friendship in action
1. Lending Harry twenty dollars
2. Borrowing Fran's car
3. Sharing your home with Michelle when her husband left

This is another way to illustrate what you think friendship means. Make each into a topic sentence and develop all three of them into separate paragraphs. (You may have four or even five meanings or examples or instances of friendship; if so, devote a paragraph to each *or* pick the three most important ones for your essay.)

By the end of a definition essay your readers should know what the word means to you. Ideally, they will have a new insight into the word, an understanding of it that they may never have had before. A good definition essay will bring home the fact that words have important meanings that are never found in the dictionary.

Example*

Here is a definition of "song," as given by one writer.

Song

Song is the most natural form of music. Issuing from within the body, it is projected by means of the most personal of all instruments, the human voice. From time immemorial, singing has been the most widespread and spontaneous way of making music.

We have in folk music a treasury of song that reflects all phases of life—work songs, love songs, drinking songs, cradle songs, patriotic songs, dance songs, songs of mourning, marching songs, play songs, narrative songs. Some are centuries old, others are of recent origin. A folk song originates with an individual, perhaps on the spur of the moment. It is taken up by others, a detail is changed, a stanza added. In the course of its wanderings it assumes a number of versions. It becomes the collective expression of a group.

One has but to listen to a love song like *Greensleeves* or *Black Is the Color of My True Love's Hair* to realize how compellingly a melody may capture the accent of tenderness and longing. Songs such as *Water Boy*, which sprang up among prisoners on the chain gang, or *Lord Randall*, with its theme of betrayal, are surcharged with emotion. Treating of basic human experience, they are understood everywhere. At the same time they are rooted in the speech rhythms, the soil, and the life of a particular place—which is why they possess the raciness and vivid local color that are among the prime attributes of folk song.

The same directness of expression is found on a more sophisticated level in the art song. Here the sentiment is more special, more sharply focused. Text and music are of known authorship, and bear the imprint of a personality. Whereas folk song usually reflects the pattern of life in rural areas, the art song issues from the culture of cities. Like the folk song, however, its musical content is shaped by man's experience and projects deeply human emotion. Schubert's famous *Serenade* has become the archetype of the love song, Brahm's *Lullaby* of the cradle song, Schumann's *Two Grenadiers* of the martial ballad. Such songs have universal appeal and exemplify the power of music to set forth the imagery of life.

*Reprinted from *The Enjoyment of Music* by Joseph Machlis, 3d ed., shorter. By permission of W. W. Norton & Company, Inc. Copyright © 1970 by W. W. Norton & Company, Inc.

Comment   Notice how the introduction leads up to the thesis sentence, and how each paragraph contributes to the total definition. The word being defined, "song," has many meanings, but the author wants to include only those that can be considered works of art. Thus, some meanings of song (popular music, rock, country) are left out.

EXERCISE 14

Write an essay giving your own definition of one of these common words:

Marriage	Deceit	Thanksgiving
Education	Anger	Satisfaction
Wisdom	Jealousy	Beauty
Love	Fear	Quiet
Bravery	Surprise	A Good Parent

Dangers in Definitions

There are certain approaches to avoid when writing definitions:

1. Never begin "According to Webster. . . ." It's been overworked.
2. Never say "Love *is when* ..." or "Truth *is when.* . . ." Write "Love *is* ..." or "Truth *is.* . . ."
3. Never confuse your audiences. If you define some difficult terms, define *all* difficult ones.
4. Never repeat the obvious at great length. We all know how the dictionary defines "love" and "fear" and "bravery." You don't need to state the same idea in your own words; what you need to do is supply your own perspective on the words. That means avoiding words that you don't have strong notions about.

Narrative

A narrative is a story. A novel is a narrative; so are many jokes. Whenever someone says, "Let me tell you what happened to me today . . . ," that person is beginning a narrative. It is no exaggeration to say that narrative is the most familiar type of communication. The classic dull school example is "My Summer Vacation." Can you think of some narratives that you have written? _____

Even if you have never written a narrative, you undoubtedly have plenty of them in your head: events that happened to you or your friends, family stories, jokes, . . . the list is endless. This chapter deals with telling those narratives. It will provide suggestions on how to write a good narrative and on how to avoid some of the problems that may arise.

The first step is to understand that narratives can sometimes seem almost too easy. There is often little thinking involved in telling a story. After all, it happened to you and you remember it, so there should not be much trouble in getting it down on paper. Yet, don't you know people who can begin a story and go on and on and on and never really get anywhere? They don't seem to know what to emphasize or how to make the point they want. The story becomes long, boring, and dull. Nobody wants to read a long, dull narrative either. The fact that many people have trouble telling even a simple story should make you suspect that narration is not so easy as it first seems.

Most important to remember is that a narrative has to have a point. Simply retelling what happened won't hold anyone's interest. The story itself has to have some purpose, some plan, some end in view. Here are five ways your narratives can get some purpose:

1. *Tell an exciting story.* Here your purpose will be to entertain or interest your audience. What makes for an exciting story? Danger, suspense, the unusual are all possibilities.
For discussion:
Can you give examples of exciting stories you have read? What made

them exciting?_____

_____

_____

2. *Illustrate a point about human nature.* Fairy tales and fables are fascinating to children (and adults, too) because they seem to speak about eternal truths. A story that makes a comment on human nature interests readers.
For discussion:
Can you give examples of such narratives? What comment or point

did they make?_____

_____

_____

3. *Make people laugh.* Real humor is probably the rarest talent. If you can tell a funny story well, you can write a good narrative essay.
For discussion:
Have you read any really funny stories? How many different kinds of

laughs can stories provide?_____

_____

_____

4. *Show how an experience dramatically changed someone's life.* All people have certain illuminating experiences, occasions when they learn something very important about themselves, other people, or the world around them. A narrative tied to such a learning experience can fascinate others.
For discussion:
Can you recall such narratives from your reading? Was it the point

or the way the point was made that most interested you?_____

_____

_____

5. *Get to the heart of a common, everyday occurrence.* If you run out of exciting events and illuminating experiences, you can still examine what happened on a certain undramatic occasion and tell what the experience meant. The most commonplace situations often give rise to such narratives; the interest lies not just in what happened, but also in your reaction, how you felt and thought. You'll be putting the reader in your place, describing your own feelings exactly.
For discussion:
Do you know of any narratives like this? Were you able to put your-

self in the writer's shoes?_____

_____

_____

These five ways of giving narratives a point are not to be thought of as separate, exclusive techniques. Feel free to use parts of each in your narratives, just as long as you keep to the central theme of your story.

PRESENTING THE NARRATIVE—THE SPEAKER

It is helpful to think of narratives as being divided into two general types: first person and third person.

First person uses "I" throughout. The person who experiences the events tells the story from his or her point of view. An autobiography is written in the first person because the author is telling the story of his or her life.

Third person uses "he," "she," or "they." The events did not happen to the writer but to the person being spoken about. Biographies are written in the third person.

You are free to use either type. Of course when you are talking about yourself, you will have to use first person, and when talking about others you will use third person (though you can present yourself as a fictitious character if you wish). Look back at the five ways of making points and see which ones *require* first person and which ones *require* third person, or whether either first person or third person can be used in any of them. _____

_____

PRESENTING THE NARRATIVE—THE ORDER

Narration demands chronological order, the order in which events happened. You can employ flashbacks, or you can backtrack a bit to fill in some detail, but the thrust of the narrative must follow the order of the events themselves. A convenient way to do this is to have each of the main-body paragraphs refer to a different stage of the story (or a stage of the speaker's perceptions). It will help if you open each paragraph with a word that signals the change from one time span to another.

Transitions of Time

These words at the beginning of your paragraphs will help your reader follow the narrative:

first	later	meanwhile
then	afterward	at the same time
next	finally	before
while	after that	earlier

PRESENTING THE NARRATIVE—THE FORM

There is no need to stick to a strict five-paragraph form in a narrative essay. You may have more than five stages to the story, but allow a paragraph for each stage. You may also want to include a short transitional paragraph to link events that have already been described to those that follow. Your narrative will have order if your point is clearly expressed in the opening or concluding paragraph and the sequence of events is clearly marked with transitional words.

PRESENTING THE NARRATIVE—THE CONCLUSION

A concluding paragraph in a narrative is a chance to tie everything together. You can tell what impressions you got from the events, or what you decided to do, or what the experience meant to you. There is no need to draw an obvious moral or give a message or sermon. The story itself should make the point you want; if the story has been told well, you will not have to hit your readers over the head with your conclusion.

Example

The First Dollar I Ever Earned

I still remember the first dollar I ever earned. I was still pretty young, about fifteen. There were never many chances for me to earn money around my neighborhood. We didn't have many supermarkets or paper routes where I could earn some money after school. My parents were more interested in my doing well in my studies than in making some pocket money to spend on candy and gum. So, by the age of fifteen, I was still looking forward to making my first money from real work. And I soon had the chance I wanted.

It was in December. I had just finished shoveling my driveway, which had been packed with eight inches of wet, heavy snow. My father came out of the door and said, "Now that you've finished here, do the driveway next door." I was mad. My neighbor had never done anything for me except say hello each time we met. I went over grudgingly.

After I had finished shoveling the driveway, I was heading toward my house when my neighbor, Mr. Rigg, called me over and said he wanted to talk to me. When I reached his steps, he pulled some money out of his pocket, telling me that I had done a good job on the driveway and that he would like me to shovel it every time it snowed. At the end of our conversation he handed me five dollars.

I was so overjoyed about that five dollars that I started making plans. The way I looked at it, every shoveling job would help make me rich. The weather report became my favorite television program, and sure enough, it snowed for several days during the next two weeks. Soon I had twenty dollars. I was so happy that I used to stay in my room and count the money over and over again and think of what to do with it.

My friends thought I was rich, because every time we went to the store I would treat them. They asked where I got the money, but I never let on. And they didn't get too nosy, for I hinted that if they found out my secret the treats would stop. It didn't take long to go through my twenty dollars; the way I spent it was probably better than any other I could have thought up, and I enjoyed every ice cream cone and box of candy I bought. I also liked being regarded as a big spender.

Now that I've grown a bit older, twenty dollars doesn't seem to excite me the way it used to. I still shovel Mr. Rigg's driveway every winter, and he still calls me over to his steps and pays me. But the thrill of earning that first dollar is gone.

Comment   This is a good student paper, a narrative that deals with the effect of a commonplace happening. You can learn from it. Look at the clear transition from one part to another. Note the use of specific details. And last of all, look at how the conclusion doesn't make too much of the incident; it simply treats it as one aspect of growing up.

EXERCISE 15

Here are some suggestions for a first-person narrative essay that presents your impression of an everyday experience. See if you can write an essay that reveals your actions and your feelings about what happened.
1. Did you ever stare at someone in a room or on a bus or train or plane? Why? What did you do when the person looked and caught you? How did you feel? What happened next?
2. Were you ever cheated? What happened? What did you do? Were you satisfied that you did the right thing? What did you learn? (Be as specific as you can.)
3. Can you remember what made you realize that you were finally growing up? How did it happen? How old were you? What were your reactions then? What do you think now?
4. What experience made you realize that someone you knew well was

getting older? Try to remember exactly how you felt at the time. Were you right? What do you think now?

5. Everyone remembers times when they said the wrong thing. Do you remember an occasion on which you said the *right* thing? What happened? What was the result?

Comparison and Contrast

Whenever you take two items and show in what ways they are alike, you are writing a *comparison*. If you show how the two are different, you are writing a *contrast*.

Comparison	Contrast
Shows similarities. Takes items that may not seem alike and points out how much they have in common. Examples: high school and college; a good dancer and a good athlete.	Shows differences. Takes items that may seem alike and shows how different they are. Examples: getting married and living together; dogs and cats.

Comparison and contrast are *techniques*, two ways of examining two different items to see how much they are alike or in what ways they differ. Suppose, for example, you were asked to explain which you liked best, movies or television. Then, in writing your essay, your *purpose* would be stated in the thesis sentence. You would say which of the two, movies or television, you preferred and tell why. The technique you would use to explain *why* would be either comparison or contrast.

Comparison and contrast are not the real reasons for writing your essay. They are only two ways of proving your point—your thesis. Keep in mind, too, that you don't have to use them constantly throughout your essay.

PLANNING THE ESSAY

Before beginning to write a comparison or a contrast essay, decide on the position you will take. The purpose of the essay should be firmly in your mind. If you are supposed to compare, say, television news and newspapers, you need to think about why. Do you want to demonstrate that television news is as good as a first-rate newpaper, or that newspapers are so bad that they're no different from television newscasts? Suppose the topic is a contrast between dogs and cats. You'll have to decide why you're comparing them. Do you wish to demonstrate that dogs are more friendly? Or do you want to prove that cats are easier to live with? As in every essay you write, the need for a main point , usually stated in the thesis sentence, is crucial.

When you are planning your essay, choose *either* comparison *or* contrast. Concentrate on similarities or on differences, not on both, because you want to keep your essay to a reasonable length. Restricting yourself to comparing or to contrasting is an important first step.

Example

Essay topic: Compare <u>or</u> contrast working and going to college

Ask yourself: Which technique is best to use in my essay? This topic is an easy one to develop by either comparison or contrast. If you think there are some ways in which working is like going to college, then you *compare* and look for similarities like these:

1. Regular schedule
2. Serious attitude necessary
3. Interesting people
4. System of rewards and punishments
5. Supervisory control
6. Always new things to learn
7. Distinctive style of dress in both
8. Chance for advancement
9. Usefulness recognized by society
10. Mental work more important than physical

Those are only some of the similarities between working in an office and going to college. Of course you can add other similarities or leave some out.

If you think working and going to college are very different, then *contrast* and look for differences such as:

1. Vacations (short versus long)
2. Clothing required (dressy versus casual)
3. Reward (money versus grades)
4. Ages (all ages versus similar ages)
5. Hours (rigid schedule versus flexible schedule)
6. Purpose (earn a living versus learning)
7. Atmosphere (commercial versus intellectual)
8. Type of work (always the same versus always new)
9. Outside activities (company picnic versus organized sports)
10. Goals (advancement in company versus earning a degree)

Once again, these are only some possible differences; you might add others and leave some out.

From the lists of similarities and differences you can see that trying to include them all in a four or five-paragraph essay would be impossible. Therefore, you have to concentrate on only one of the lists, either the similarities or the differences. When you have made up your mind which to choose, select the most important ones *for you*. Those are the points you will stress; you can leave out the less important ones or refer to them briefly, but you will focus on the key points that you think matter most.

In every paper you write you will not have to go through such an extensive process of searching around for similarities or differences. You will probably have enough if you think of only three or four and jot them down. But the lists you have just read do show that almost every topic has many possibilities for comparison and contrast. Your job now is to limit those possibilities to the ones that seem most important to you. Once you have done that, you are ready to decide which order to choose.

ORDERING THE ESSAY

Once you have decided on a comparison (similarities) or contrast (differences) and have listed the points you want to stress, you are almost ready to begin the essay. First, though, you have to choose how to present your material. There are two basic approaches: a paragraph for each major characteristic, or a paragraph for each item being compared or contrasted.

Ordering by Characteristics

This approach requires a separate paragraph for each characteristic. The general outline of such an essay, done in terms of work and college, will be as follows:

Par.   I. Introduction
Par. II. Scheduling (how work and college are alike or different)
Par. III. People (how work and college are alike or different)
Par. IV. Goals (how work and college are alike or different)
Par. V. Conclusion

If you wanted to add other characteristics like atmosphere or dress requirements, you would devote an entire paragraph to each.

Ordering by Item

This approach calls for two longer main body paragraphs, one for each item being compared or contrasted.

Par. I.   Introduction
Par. II. Work (its scheduling, the people there, the goals, the atmosphere, and so on)
Par. III. College (its scheduling, the people there, the goals, the atmosphere, and so on)
Par. IV.   Conclusion

Here are the two approaches worked out in terms of automobiles:

Characteristics

    Par.   I. Introduction
              Thesis sentence: Fords and Chevys are different (or similar).
    Par. II. Economy
              A. Ford
              B. Chevrolet
    Par. III. Style
              A. Ford
              B. Chevrolet
    Par. IV. Durability
              A. Ford
              B. Chevrolet
    Par. V. Conclusion

You can see right away that the number of characteristics you choose determines the number of main body paragraphs you have to write.

Items

    Par.   I. Introduction
              Thesis sentence: Fords and Chevys are different (or similar).
    Par. II. Ford
              A. Economy
              B. Style
              C. Durability
    Par. III. Chevrolet
              A. Economy
              B. Style
              C. Durability
    Par. IV. Conclusion

The number of main-body paragraphs is determined by the number of items being compared or contrasted. If you wanted to include Plymouths, you would need a separate paragraph to discuss Plymouths in terms of economy, style, and durability.

KEEPING MATTERS CLEAR

As you write your essay, make sure you introduce each difference or similarity at the opening of your paragraphs so that there is no chance for your readers (or you) to get confused. When you switch to another topic in a new paragraph, use transitional opening words to emphasize your points.

Useful Transitional Words and Phrases

on one hand . . . on the other hand	similarly
both . . . and	in contrast
this . . . that	on the contrary
formerly . . . at present	however
long ago . . . now	nevertheless
now . . . then	furthermore

THE CONCLUSION

Use the conclusion to make your choice clear, or to reinforce the most important reason for your comparison. Or, you may want to add that the topics you have been dealing with are not *totally* different, nor are they *exactly* alike. The point of your essay is not to convince your readers of *absolute* similarities or differences; you simply want to show them that you see real opportunities for making a choice or a comparison.

Example*

Here is a paragraph that contrasts different kinds of pizza.

The Best Pizza

The Spot, 163 Wooster Street, New Haven. Texture is the key to superlative pizza. Most good pizzerias (for example, the Shakey's chain and Goldberg's in New York) distinguish themselves on flavor and foolishly accept the conventional up-from-Chef-Boy-Ar-Dee texture. At the Spot, the crust is thick and sinewy, imposing its presence on the chewer rather than meshing unassertively with the rest of the goop.

Comment   Notice how the writers set the terms of contrast right at the opening. They came right out and said that "texture" is the "key," the feature that separates the good from the best. The approach used here is "by characteristic."

Example

Here is a longer essay that contrasts two items from three viewpoints.

There are two completely different types of college experiences available: living at school and living at home. For both, the courses, professors, assignments, and buildings are the same. It's quite possible to get an equally good education from one as from the other. Nevertheless, there are many more advantages to living away than there are to staying at home.

Students who live at college become more a part of the school. It is their second home for four very important years. College becomes a world in itself, removed from the normal routine and set aside totally for learning. In

---

*Reprinted with the permission of Farrar, Straus & Giroux, Inc., from *The Best* by Peter Passell and Leonard Ross. Copyright © 1974 by Peter Passell and Leonard Ross, p. 90.

contrast, students living at home cannot get into the world of college because they are not there long enough; it's only one part of their lives. In
many ways, it's still like high school, with activities determined by the needs
of the family, while those living at college have more freedom, thanks to
living in a dormitory, fraternity house, or apartment.

The freedom of living at school builds social maturity. Of course there are
the usual silly activities—dormitory pranks, football rallies, and all the rest.
But at college there is a wider world full of new, unknown people. Getting
into that world isn't always easy, but the experience helps students grow.
Students living at home, on the other hand, miss out on such opportunities.
They are dealing, most of the time, with people they have always known:
family, relatives, high school friends. There isn't enough chance to keep up
with new friends because it's back home again when classes end.

Most important of all, living at school is better intellectually. If school is
a learning experience, the more of it the better. Class discussions can be
carried over to dinner or a late-night bull session. Other students in the
dorm can answer difficult questions or supply missed lecture notes. The
library is a short walk away. At school, everyone feels part of a new learning
experience; they all reinforce each other's feeling of being there to find out
new ideas and meet new people. Students who live at home don't have these
advantages. They have no one there who can share their experience or talk
about what came up in class. Studying is difficult at home because of the
noise and because there is no library nearby.

Living away, then, has great advantages. It gives a student a fuller college experience and makes learning a large part of his or her life, but the
student living at home commutes to school as if going to work. The student
at home saves money, for living away isn't cheap, even though campus jobs
and loans are usually available. But the extra expense of living away is
worth it, for it offers the opportunity to get a better, fuller education.

Comment   Again, the development here is "by characteristic," and
there are as many paragraphs as there are points of difference. Note how
the introduction ends with a clear thesis sentence, and how the conclusion anticipates disagreement, turning it into a "final" statement that
rounds out the essay.

EXERCISE 16

Write an essay comparing *or* contrasting one of the following sets. Base
your paper on at least *three* similarities or differences.
  1. High school and college (be specific about which ones)
  2. Transportation as it now is and as it used to be
  3. Getting married and living together
  4. Old people and infants
  5. Life in the country and life in the city (be specific)
  6. Vacations in summer and vacations in winter
  7. The book and the movie made from it
  8. Your town (city) now and five years ago

9. The way you view college now and the way you viewed it five years ago
10. Mental work and physical labor (pick specific types of each)

Argument

Every paragraph and essay you write will be a form of persuasion, an attempt to convince your readers that your thesis is true. But there is a special type of writing that persuades by means of solid, sensible, *logical* arguments. When writing an argument essay, draw attention to your purpose by stating it in the beginning. A good way to state your point of view is to have your thesis sentence contain the words "should," "ought," or "must."

Examples
These thesis sentences would begin argument essays:
1. There ought to be more recreational facilities for Baytown's teenagers.
2. Public places (restaurants, meeting rooms, and so on) should have separate smoking sections.
3. Automobile manufacturers must build cars that use less gas.

Every one of these thesis sentences states the argument clearly. The readers know exactly where the writer stands, and they will expect that the rest of the essay will back up the thesis sentence with good, logical arguments.

The thesis sentence of an argument essay presents what you believe. The rest of the essay shows the readers why they should believe what you believe. You do this by supplying good reasons that will convince them. Your goal is to get them to agree with you about an issue that has two sides; you want them on your side, not with the opposition.

HOW READERS BECOME CONVINCED

Just because you have a strong belief does not mean that you can convince your readers. Many people believe deeply in what seem like crazy ideas or notions. They will never persuade anyone simply on the *strength* of their convictions, but they may win followers through good solid arguments and reasons.

BELIEF	Goes in the thesis sentence
ARGUMENT	Backs up belief with proof

Readers can be convinced if you give them facts, statistics, and statements of expert opinion. Suppose you want to argue that class attendance should be voluntary. You might use these three kinds of evidence to back up your opinion.

> *Facts:* Seven students passed the final exam in Biology 141 but failed the course because of poor attendance.

This fact demonstrates that you are not merely offering your own opinion but that you have specific information to prove your thesis.

> *Statistics:* Infirmary records show that the average student is sick for three school days each term.

No reader will question that because it can be easily verified

> *Expert Opinion:* Dean Scholes says that the final examination is the single best test of someone's knowledge of a course.

The Dean, of course, is one of the best-known authorities about college, so her opinion is valuable.

HOW TO REGARD YOUR AUDIENCE

Think of your readers as intelligent, reasonable people who do not yet agree with you. They have open minds, but are unlikely to be persuaded without sufficient evidence. They demand proof or sound reasons for agreeing with you. Your job is to convince them by the logic of your arguments and the quality of your examples. Your emphasis must be on good sense, not emotion.

PREPARING TO WRITE AN ARGUMENT ESSAY

Think of your main arguments in advance. It is also wise to think of the arguments *against* you as well. If you know what the opposition believes, you should look for weaknesses in these anti-arguments as you write.

Example

Topic: Capital Punishment Should Be Abolished

Arguments For	*Arguments Against*
1. Killing is immoral.	1. The Bible approves "an eye for an eye."
2. Mistakes can be made.	2. Very few mistakes are made.
3. It is no deterrent.	3. It is a deterrent.

Now you can write your essay, knowing in advance what your opponents can say against your point. You are also in a better position to evaluate the quality of your own arguments in relation to the arguments against them. Perhaps you will have discovered that you have an ironclad case in one of your three arguments; that would be the one to stress as the most important, and probably should be placed last for extra emphasis.

EXERCISE 17

For each of the following five topics, list three arguments on the "for" side and three on the "against" side:

1. *Topic:* Legalizing marijuana

For	*Against*
1. _____	1. _____
_____	_____
2. _____	2. _____
_____	_____
3. _____	3. _____
_____	_____

2. *Topic:* Only people who have passed a literacy test should be allowed to vote.

For	*Against*
1. _____	1. _____
_____	_____
2. _____	2. _____
_____	_____
3. _____	3. _____
_____	_____

3. *Topic:* There should be a limit to how much money a person can have.

For	*Against*
1. _____	1. _____
_____	_____
2. _____	2. _____
_____	_____

3. _____   3. _____

_____   _____

4. *Topic:* Couples should live together before getting married.

For	*Against*

1. _____   1. _____

_____   _____

2. _____   2. _____

_____   _____

3. _____   3. _____

_____   _____

5. *Topic:* Students who work hard in a course ought to pass.

For	*Against*

1. _____   1. _____

_____   _____

2. _____   2. _____

_____   _____

3. _____   3. _____

_____   _____

There are four questions your audience wants answered.
1. What is the problem? (How serious is it?)
2. Why should we accept your solution?
3. How can the change be made?
4. What will be the result of doing as you say?
If you are satisfied that you have good answers to these tough questions, you are ready to write.

HANDLING ARGUMENTS IN YOUR ESSAY

Order the reasons   In a five-paragraph essay you will have three good reasons for believing in your side of the issue. The most important point *should never be second.* Put it at the beginning or, even better, at the end, and draw attention to it by saying "Most important of all," or "The main reason."

An alternative arrangement of an essay is to have four paragraphs: one long main-body paragraph that attacks your opponents' reasons (fairly, through logic) and another long main-body paragraph that presents your own reasons. (There will be an introduction and conclusion too, of course.)

Make concessions Admit that your opponent has some good points, and that your case is not completely airtight. You will be saying that, even with its problems, your argument is better than any alternative. By anticipating disagreements, you can modify your audience's reaction to them, and you will also seem fairer if you bring up some weak points of your own argument. Words introducing a concession might be: "although," "even though," "even if," "I admit," or "despite."

Be fair The readers want a sensible argument; they will not be convinced by name calling, slanting the facts, or deliberate distortions. They also will detect any appeals to their emotions without good reason. If you are unfair, your whole essay will suffer because the audience will not trust anything you write.

Example
Television Is Bad for Children

By the time children reach school, they have spent up to one-third of their waking hours in front of the television. The enormous influence of TV programs is just beginning to be realized, and we're finding out that most of the effect is bad. Far too much of a child's time is completely wasted by so much television. It's time that we understand the bad effects television can have on little children.

One reason TV watching is bad is that it forces kids into becoming consumers and then tricks them. They get bombarded by ads for dangerous toys, mindless games, and unhealthful foods. They force their parents to buy them, even though many parents are learning that the products advertised on TV are not always worthwhile. The children themselves are not wise enough to detect the falsity of so much advertising. They're too gullible, so they're a perfect target for the hucksters peddling their wares when kids are watching.

Another bad effect of television watching is that kids are overexposed to violence. They watch hours of murders, fights, and crime every week, with no adult around to tell them that life isn't like that most of the time. Even cartoon shows are offenders; think of how much fighting goes on in *Bugs Bunny* or *Road Runner*, even though it's all in fun. The effect of the heavy dose of violence is to suggest to kids that violence is an ordinary way of life, and that slugging, shooting, and cheating are ways to succeed. Is that what parents want their children to learn?

Most important of all, kids watching TV are passive. They just sit back and let things happen to them, willing to be entertained rather than finding their own ways of amusing themselves. Children are inventive; they have the ability to imagine a whole world of their own, turning a street into a baseball field or a chair into a rocket ship. But what happens when their imaginations aren't needed, when TV does all the imagining for them? Obviously, these kids are not going to grow up as inventive and imaginative as their parents, for they have been robbed of creative impulses by television watching.

The total effect of most TV is dangerous. Leading educators say that this does not mean that programs like *Sesame Street* and some of the best cartoon shows are wrong and should be stopped. But it does mean that kids are being exposed to too much bad TV, and their characters are being shaped by the worst kinds of forces in our society. It's time for parents to take charge and supervise their children's play, and to engage in activities with their children instead of parking them by the tube and hoping it will act as a baby sitter. The influence of TV is so important that parents will have to be on their guard at all times in order to make sure their children are not being harmed by exposure to it.

Comment   The use of transitional words at the beginning of each main-body paragraph helps the reader switch from one idea to the next, and also follow the writer's train of thought right up to the "most important of all" reason that's placed last for added emphasis. The conclusion helps persuade you to accept the writer's argument by taking into account the opposition's claim that *Sesame Street* could hardly be considered harmful, according to leading educators.

TYPES OF ARGUMENTS TO AVOID

Among the many different ways of persuading your reader are some trick appeals based on false reasoning. This kind of reasoning seems all right when you first hear or read it. But if you think about it, you'll find that it is illogical and foolish. Many of these trick appeals are based on natural human emotions.

Appeal to pride   An appeal to pride convinces the audience by attaching prestige to the argument. The message is that you ought to agree because Princess X or Fullback Y or Film Star Z agrees. This is a fallacy. Just because these famous people do it says nothing about its rightness or wrongness.

Examples

Baseball Player Q drinks Brand X, so you should too.
Senator L believes in harsh prison sentences, so you should too.

Bandwagon effect   The bandwagon effect attempts to show the overwhelming popularity of the idea. The message is that if everyone is doing it, it must be right. But, of course, the value of something is not necessarily related to how many people do it.

Examples

Brand A is the largest selling car in America.
Everyone cheats a little, so it can't be bad.

Appeal to fear   The appeal to fear threatens the audience with evil consequences. It's an emotional plea, not one based on solid reasons. It works on the feelings without ever demonstrating how the evil results will come about. "Scare tactics" is another term for this appeal.

Examples

If you don't buy this toothpaste, you won't get any dates.
Unless the voters have more freedom, the country will be taken over by extremists.

Name calling Name calling attempts to discredit the opposition by associating them with distasteful characters and ideas. There is never any attempt to *prove* that opponents deserve the name they are being called.

Examples

The plan to let everyone decide about where to put the road sounds like Communism to me. (No proof offered.)
That teacher acted just like a dictator. (No proof offered.)

EXERCISE 18

Identify the type of false argument being used in each of these sentences.
1. Everyone else on the block has a swimming pool.

2. If the city doesn't build more parks, crime will increase.

3. The President has a dog in the White House, so everyone else should have one too.

4. This plan has been tried all over the country, so we should try it here.

5. All I can say is that her idea is simple-minded.

EXERCISE 19

Some of the following sentences contain good support for arguments. Mark them with an X in the margin.

1. _____ My Uncle Sandy is divorced, so don't pay any attention to his advice.

2. _____ Everyone knows that hard work always brings good results.

3. _____ If you use the deodorant suggested by Rita Meter, the famous beauty adviser, you'll get more dates.

4. _____ The police department reports that serious crimes have dropped ten percent in the last year.

5. _____ I once had a bad hamburger at Fred's Restaurant, so I will never go back again.

6. _____ Since Alice Appelson's last novel was good, her next one will be good too.

7. _____ The movie is so interesting that it's bound to be a hit.

8. _____ My roommate never studies but passes all his courses, so I can follow his example and do just as well.

9. _____ Shakespeare is boring; everybody in the class says so.

10. _____ I know Allen never goes on dates because he's never asked Sheila out.

EXERCISE 20

Write an argument essay on one of these topics:
1. Grades should/should not be abolished.
2. The federal government should/should not ban pornography.
3. Drug pushers should/should not be executed.
4. Movies are/are not too violent.
5. The "American Dream" is/is not dead.
6. Racism is still a major problem in _____. (Yes or No?)
7. Teenagers today have too much freedom. (Yes or No?)
8. Teachers should be judged on how well their classes do. (Yes or No?)
9. Women's sports in school should get as much money as men's. (Yes or No?)
10. As soon as a person gets a full-time job, he or she should move away from home. (Yes or No?)

CHAPTER 3

A WRITER'S CONCERNS

The Writer's Point of View

It is often useful to think of writing in terms of who is addressing whom. The words that apply are *speaker*, *audience*, and *occasion*.

SPEAKER . . . . does the writing
AUDIENCE . . . . does the reading
OCCASION . . . . the reason for writing

Think of a love letter. The speaker is the one who wrote it; the audience is the one it was intended for; and the occasion is, perhaps, a birthday, anniversary, or just the desire to keep in touch. But suppose the writer knew that someone else (say a friend, a sister, or brother of the recipient) were to read the letter. Would it be written the same way as if it were for the loved one's eyes alone? Probably not, and the reason for the difference has to do with audience. The letter would no longer be for the loved one *exclusively*, so certain feelings would be put differently. What do you think would change? List some differences in the tone, the style, the details.

Only the loved one will see it:

_____

_____

Others will see it:

_____

_____

Take another example of how the audience can play a large role. Suppose you had to write a recommendation for a friend and you knew the person who would be reading the letter. Would your letter read the same as if it were addressed to a stranger at a large, impersonal corporation? One more question: suppose you knew that the person you were recommending would see the letter. How would that affect what you say?

From these two examples it becomes clear that the type of writing and the style of writing depend on who is expected to read it (audience) and the circumstances that give rise to the writing (occasion). The writer changes, adopts new and different postures and even personalities, depending on who is listening. That this happens isn't surprising when you consider how many different shades of personality and language every person projects to friends, parents, lovers, officials, co-workers, and strangers. If you talk and act differently to different types of people (though the differences may often be only slight), it is reasonable to expect that you will carry the same distinctions over into writing.

It is important to emphasize that the switches a person makes have nothing to do with being hypocritical. There are simply different vocabularies and different styles to use so that a particular audience will understand what you are saying. You can test this yourself: think of the different ways you would explain the plot of a movie to (a) a close friend; (b) a parent or relative; (c) a teacher. Surely you would not change around what actually happened in the film, but you would use very different words and make some changes of emphasis. The same would apply in a description of a date you had, or a fight you saw, or a trip you took. It is perfectly normal to make such switches so that your meaning will be clear. This chapter will help you use them in order to make better essays.

POINT OF VIEW

For a composition course, and for most of the writing you will be doing in college, you can assume that the speaker/audience/occasion relationship will be like this:

SPEAKER   Someone interested in the topic. (*You*)
AUDIENCE   Others who are interested in what you have to write. They are slightly skeptical, but they are willing to be convinced and want proof.
OCCASION   You have decided that you have some points to make about a particular subject.

HOW TO CHARACTERIZE YOURSELF

You, of course, will be the speaker. But which you? Which side of yourself will you project? Angry? Concerned? Funny? Rational? Interested? Pugnacious? It all depends on what you think will work best. The important fact to realize is that *some* side of you will come across, and it is wise to control the impression the reader gets. You are in command, and if you want to project one particular side of your personality, then do so, just as long as you are consistent and thorough.

In the most common type of essay the speaker is projected as the one who is interested, informed, rational, and alert to the possibilities of the subject. If you choose this approach, there are four guidelines to follow:

1. Never protest that you don't know much about your topic.
2. Never pretend to be an expert when you are not. These two guidelines seem to contradict each other, but they don't when you reflect on them. If you don't know much on a topic, you shouldn't be writing on it. But at the same time no one expects you to be the world's leading expert on the subject, and it will never hurt to admit that you don't know everything.
3. Don't be afraid to say "I think," or "it seems to me," or "as far as I can tell." Label your guesses as guesses. (Don't overdo this either: "In my opinion I feel that he appeared happy about his promotion" sounds silly.)
4. Don't expect to say everything on the topic in just five paragraphs. Even the narrowest of topics cannot be fully explored in a brief essay; you are aiming for a sharply focused thesis about the topic, not exhaustive coverage.

HOW TO REGARD YOUR AUDIENCE

You will usually be addressing your fellow students and your instructor. Use common sense when you pick a thesis. Do not set out to prove what they already believe (Freedom Is Wonderful, Life Is Funny) or to explain what they already know (The Rules of Checkers, Money Is Important). Assume that your audience is already interested in what you have to say, but needs to be convinced. They won't believe you just because you sound sincere. (If you wanted to trick someone, wouldn't you try to sound as sincere as possible?)

HOW FORMAL TO BE

Good writing comes in all shapes and sizes, in all types and styles. There are no absolutely firm rules about how formal or informal you should be, but there are suggestions and warnings.

First of all, your readers are used to getting their information from printed sources: books, newspapers, reports, magazines, letters, and memos. Your essay will be another form of information, so it's best to model your style on the kind of writing your readers are accustomed to. When you do public writing addressed to a relatively large group, your essays should sound more formal than a note to a friend or a diary. Therefore your essay will probably be a bit more formal than what you are used to writing and more like what you are used to *reading*. Keep in mind these useful distinctions between formal writing and casual writing:

More Formal Writing	*More Casual Writing*
No unintentional slang	Slang
No abbreviations	Abbreviations
Smooth flow of sentences	Pauses and switches
Coherent paragraphs	Loose paragraphs
Strict attention to spelling, grammar, and usage	Little attention to the fine points of spelling, grammar, and usage
No chatty style	Chatty style

Think of these as contrasts of style, with your essays tending toward formal writing. You might prefer to be more formal or less formal, but it is never advisable to sound very chatty or overly casual.

Examples

Too formal

It is definitely to be wished that the high school student of today assume a studious attitude toward scholastic endeavors. Such an attitude, properly maintained, will repay the student many times over in an increase of knowledge.

This is stiff, pompous writing, full of dead words and fancy-sounding sentences.

Too chatty

You know, kids in high school nowadays could study some more. They'd find out more stuff if they hit the books.

This is the other extreme, far too casual for a college essay.

More suitable

Today's high school students would learn more if they spent more time studying.

Notice that the most suitable passage makes its point in fewer words. It's more economical as well as more appropriate.

EXERCISE 1

Write paragraphs that *illustrate* a proverb. Do three versions of the same topic: one very stiff and formal, one very loose and chatty, and one in a style appropriate for a college essay. Some suggested topics are:

1. A bird in the hand is worth two in the bush.
2. A penny saved is a penny earned.
3. Too many cooks spoil the broth.
4. Many hands make light work.
5. Don't cross your bridge until you come to it.

EXERCISE 2

The new coffee table you ordered from Drake's Department Store arrived yesterday, but when you opened the crate you found that it had only three legs. When you called to complain, the furniture manager told you to put your complaint in writing, giving all the details. Write that account now in short essay form. When you write, choose how you will come across; pick *one* of these "characters" and stick to it:

    A. Furious
    B. Nasty
    C. Weak
    D. Bewildered
    E. Disappointed

Give details to back up your response.

EXERCISE 3

Write two separate paragraphs describing a city or vacation spot you know well. Aim each paragraph at a different type of reader chosen from the following list:

    A. A close friend your age who shares your interests
    B. A visitor your age from another country
    C. An elderly aunt or uncle
    D. A young nephew or niece

After writing, note which details and points of style changed as you wrote to a different audience.

Revising and Proofreading

Professional writers never sit down and turn out a perfect essay all at once. They write and rewrite through a long, sometimes difficult process in order to produce the best possible article or essay, one that says exactly what they want. Some of the steps a professional takes can benefit any writer.

THE FIRST DRAFT

You may often find that when you have written the first draft of your essay, it doesn't sound right, or it doesn't say what you had planned. Don't be surprised; it happens all the time. The first draft rarely turns out to be the finished product. Be prepared to do some revising. That means crossing out, drawing arrows from one point to another, rearranging paragraphs, adding supporting details, reworking language to make it more concrete, and maybe even performing major surgery by cutting, transferring, and pasting sentences in other places.

REVISING

When the first draft is done, consider the following three points in your revision process.

The thesis Are you trying to prove something that would take a whole book to prove? Do all your paragraphs back up the one point made in the thesis sentence? It may be that you have wandered away from the thesis sentence and found a new, more interesting approach. You might even discover that you no longer believe what you said in the thesis sentence. That is all to the good, for your first draft has put you closer in touch with your real opinions and ideas. Revise the essay to take them into account.

Paragraph structure Does each paragraph have a single main idea? Does that main idea clearly relate to the thesis sentence? Does each paragraph have enough supporting detail to back up the topic? Can you think of better examples? If so, revise, adding extra examples and details. (If you find that some main-body paragraphs have only three or four sentences, you should suspect that there aren't enough details to support your points.)

Sentences Do all the sentences follow the same dull pattern? Do they often begin with the same words? Can some be combined? Do you use the verb "be" ("am," "is," "are" "was") too often? Can concrete language replace ordinary words? Are your sentences clear, with good grammar and usage? Or do you find fragments and run-ons?

REWRITING

The revising stage involved crossing out and changing; rewriting involves producing the best possible copy, neatly written (or typed, if you can do it). Once you have rewritten the paper to your satisfaction, you are ready to move on to the next step, proofreading.

PROOFREADING

The word "proofreading" refers to what you do when you have finished writing your final draft. You need to read the paper over to check for mistakes. These mistakes will not be in ideas or paragraph development, which you corrected in the revision process.

In proofreading, look for oversights: misspelling, faulty punctuation, incorrect capitalization, and words left out. Everyone makes careless mistakes, but good writers find them before the final draft is submitted. Proofreading is not exciting, but it is necessary if all the work you did on the essay is to pay off.

Save plenty of time   It's best to put your rewritten paper away for a while and come back to it fresh for a final proofreading. That way you will be able to see it with new eyes and perhaps spot mistakes that slipped by.

Read the paper as slowly as possible   You may not think you're a speedy reader, but when it comes to you own work you are. You rush through it because you already know what is in it. But you should be looking for careless errors, slips of the pen. You will never find them unless you read word by word, sometimes even letter by letter. (For bad cases of carelessness, one technique is to put a pencil dot under every letter to force the eye to go slowly.)

Read the paper out loud   Sometimes, by saying aloud every word, you can see what is missing. (But this won't work if you read too fast; again, reading slowly is the key.)

Have a friend read the paper to you   Another set of eyes can remove many errors.

Know what you usually get wrong   Do you confuse "its" and "it's"? Then look carefully every time you see them in your paper. Do you have trouble with the "s" endings of verbs? Then look at every verb and decide whether it needs one. Your instructor's comments and markings on previous essays are the best guide to your problem areas. Keep lists of (a) spelling problems (there is space for a list on the inside back cover of this book); (b) particular problems with grammar and usage. The problems are guaranteed to remain with you unless you make an attempt to cope with them. The first step toward coping is to know where the trouble lies.

EXERCISE 4

Revise and proofread the following paragraphs. Write in the corrections directly above the line.

I got my frist job thorough my confesser. A gentle old priest who regarded me as a very saintly boy. And regularly aksed me to pray for his intention. If innocence and sanctity are realted, he was probably no so far wrong about me because oncet I confessed to "bad thoughts, meaning, I suppose, murderering my Grandmother, but Father O'Regan intrepreted it differently, and their ensued an agonizing few minute's in witch he aksed me questiones I did'nt understand, and I gave him answers that he did'nt understand, and I suspect that when I left the confession box, the poor man was as shaken as I was.*

Person who live in suburbs or rural locations can enjoy bird watching right at home, planting shrubes and Evergreens for shelter and providing food an water will attract som species in large numbers, and a much larger variety in small numbers. Many observer has identified 50 or more species in a suburbian yeard. A window feeder and a bird bath with dripping water will bring into view birds that might otherways stay in the shrubbery.**

---

*Adapted from Frank O'Connor, *An Only Child* (London: Macmillan, Ltd.), p. 130.
**Adapted from *Birds of North America* by Chandler S. Robins, Bertel Bruun, and Herbert S. Zim. © Copyright 1966 by Western Publishing Company, Inc. Used by permission.

CHAPTER 4

SENTENCE SENSE

Sentences and Fragments

Every sentence needs a *subject* and a *verb*.

VERB

Verbs are words that change to show time.

sink	walk	*am, is, are*
sank	walk*ed*	*was, were*
sunk		*been*

Verbs can provide the action of the sentence or they can link ideas together:

Action: She *fired* the gun.
Linking: She *is* a good shot.

Look for verbs in the verb slot of the sentence:

The men _____ here.

A friend _____ kind.

Words that fit into those blanks are verbs.

EXERCISE 1

Underline the verbs in the following sentences:
1. Felix the Cat is his favorite cartoon character.
2. The plane dived toward the water.
3. Overhead, high above the stadium, the scoreboard flashed a rainbow of brilliant colors.
4. I asked her for the time.
5. Albertine cracked a smile at the spectators on the boardwalk.
6. Thunder and lightning filled the evening sky.
7. The mountain trail suddenly became steep.
8. On Saturday afternoons, Tom takes a long nap.
9. Where are my new fishing rods?
10. The speech delighted the huge audience.

Verbals

Words that end in "-ing" (present participles) or are preceded by "to" (infinitives) look very much like verbs but cannot, by themselves, serve as verbs. They can become verbs only when a helping verb (auxiliary) is added to them. The following examples are not sentences because they do not have a complete verb:

> ...I *walking* to the store ...(present participle)
> ...I *to walk* to the store ...(infinitive)

There is something missing—a helping verb:

I *WAS walking* to the store.
I *USED to walk* to the store.

Now they are complete sentences. In both, the verb is made up of more than one word.

EXERCISE 2

Some of the following sentences need helping verbs. Write them in above the line where needed.
1. My sister and her friend Norma trying to climb over the barbed-wire fence.
2. The old woman striding across the bridge.
3. The jet flying overhead is new.
4. Other citizens deciding to do what they can about the issue.
5. The town government not really willing to improve the water supply.
6. Many older people living in poverty.
7. The track star sitting in the third row of the plane.
8. The electricity to generate power for factories.

9. The sirens and flashing lights alarming all the sleepy apartment dwellers.
10. Arlene to dance tonight in *The Nutcracker*.

SUBJECT

The subject is the answer to the question "Who?" or "What?" before the verb.

We want to go.	Q.	WHO wants to go?
	A.	We
	SUBJECT	We

It died.	Q.	WHAT died?
	A.	It
	SUBJECT	It

Look for the subject in the subject slot in the sentence.

_____must stick together.

_____is kind.

In questions, the subject comes after the verb or between the parts of the verb; the same holds true for sentences beginning with "There are":

Did _____ ask her?

There are _____ for staying.

Any word or group of words that will fit into those slots will be the subject.
The subject of a sentence can be a NOUN:

My *uncle* drives a Pontiac.

It can be a PRONOUN:

He lives in Wyoming.

Or it can be a longer phrase:

Living in the country is becoming popular.
To become a pilot was her ambition.

EXERCISE 3

Underline the subjects in the following sentences:
1. They all liked to run.
2. All of them liked to run.
3. The clouds around Jupiter are visible through a good telescope.
4. Talking in the library is forbidden.

5. In the eighteenth century, to climb a mountain was regarded as the height of folly.
6. It costs about six thousand dollars.
7. After dinner, he tidied up and began listening to the radio.
8. Spectators are forbidden in the arena on Tuesdays.
9. What kind of plates did you get?
10. The money was divided among seven children.

NOUNS

A noun changes to show number, either one or many:

ma**n**	house	mo*u*se	hope	admonition
me**n**	house**s**	mi*c*e	hope**s**	admonition**s**

(A few nouns stay the same: deer, moose.)

Nouns can be preceded by the words "a" ("an" if they begin with a vowel sound: a, e, i, o, u) or "the." Nouns supply names for people, places, things, and ideas.

PRONOUNS

A pronoun can replace a noun. Whenever a noun appears as subject, a pronoun can substitute for it.

Ms. Kern shopped yesterday. (noun)
She shopped yesterday.   (pronoun)

Pronouns are among the most frequently used words; when they serve as subjects, they are just as good as nouns in making the sentence complete. For instance, these two sentences are equally correct:

The little *boy* fell.
He fell.

Even though you may not know who the "he" is, the sentence is a complete one. Further explanations about the "he" might have come in the previous sentence, or may appear in the next one. So even though a pronoun does not always convey as much information as the noun it stands for, it is fully capable of serving as subject for any sentence.

DEPENDENT CLAUSES

Dependent clauses are groups of words that may be mistaken for complete sentences. They *depend* on other groups of words for their full meaning and so must be attached to complete sentences. These are *dependent* clauses:

...*when* I was in sixth grade ...

...*if* the tennis court is dry ...
.. *after* the bus driver fainted ...
...*since* the paint is still wet ...
...*because* all her evening shoes were still lying unopened in the green
    trunk upstairs ...
...*that* I liked her ...

All these clauses have subjects and verbs, but they also have words in front of them that point to sentences. They must be attached to those sentences; dependent clauses cannot stand by themselves.

One of the most common errors is to mistake a dependent clause for a real sentence and begin it with a capital letter and end it with a period. This clause—mistaken for a sentence—is called a *sentence fragment*. All unintentional fragments are serious problems. (A fragment can also be caused by the lack of a subject or verb.)

You can eliminate many sentence fragments by knowing the difference between a dependent clause and a complete sentence. The words that begin a dependent clause can serve to warn you:

Because	Unless	Who	Why
If	Until	What	How
Although	While	When	That
After	Since	Where	Which

When these words begin a sentence, there *must* be a comma after them, followed by a subject and verb.*

Example

Unless I am mistaken, the text has six hundred pages.

    dependent clause   subject verb

EXERCISE 4

Some of the items below are complete sentences; mark them with an S. *Some* of the items are fragments; mark them with an F.

1. _____Trying to light a campfire in the pouring rain.

2. _____After allowing for all possible errors, he still concluded that the gold was worth at least one hundred thousand dollars.

3. _____Delighted to be in Acapulco, a place she had always wanted to see after hearing about it from friends for the past ten years.

4. _____The kind of person who never talks about you behind your back or says anything about you to others that she would not say to you herself.

*This does not apply when the words in the two columns on the right begin questions.

5. _____The uncle of the woman who lives on the farm.

6. _____Like taking elevators and having to get stuck in traffic on the way to work.

7. _____While Bruno was out with a cold, the manager replaced him with a new counterman.

8. _____The kind of mileage you are looking for in an economy car nowadays.

9. _____Only after eleven in the morning.

10. _____To be able to say that you tried as hard as you could in spite of every difficulty.

Complete sentences rarely begin with these words:

Who		
Whose	(except for	Such as
Which	questions)	Especially

When beginning with "for example" or "for instance," be especially careful to include a subject and verb.

TO FIX A SENTENCE FRAGMENT

Most fragments are caused by stopping too soon:

> He used to hate his Aunt Bertha. Because she made him take out the garbage and scrub the kitchen floor.

The first sentence is complete, but the second is a fragment. You ask, "What happened because she made him do those chores?" The answer is, as we already know, contained in the first sentence. To correct the fragment, remove the period and the next capital letter. The sentence is now complete because it is made up of a smaller sentence and a dependent clause:

> He used to hate his Aunt Bertha because she made him take out the garbage and scrub the kitchen floor.

Fix most sentence fragments by connecting them to adjoining sentences and removing the period and capital letter around the dependent clause.

EXAMPLE

> I walked along the beach. And found seashells. Displaying beautifully varied colors. Which started reminding me of sights I loved.

This passage has four sentences, or so it seems. Let's look more closely:

I walked along the beach.	Verb: walked Subject: I Sentence: YES
And found seashells.	Verb: found Subject: NO (a FRAGMENT) Solution: link it to the previous sentence.
Displaying beautifully varied colors.	Verb: NO. The "-ing" words need helping verbs to complete them. (a FRAGMENT; link it to the previous sentence)
Which started reminding me of sights I loved.	Verb: started Subject: Which *Dependent clause*: Which (a FRAGMENT; link it to the previous sentence)

So, the corrected passage would read:

I walked along the beach and found seashells displaying beautifully varied colors which started reminding me of sights I loved.

The whole passage has become one long sentence that could not be broken up at any point without creating a fragment.

Try the rest of the paragraph:

One had a pale orange tint. Another a purple that looked like the last rays of a sunset. A third was creamy white. Like the color of a genuine pearl.

EXERCISE 5

Take the passage and find the fragments.Then rewrite it correctly; do not add or remove words.

_____

_____

_____

_____

EXERCISE 6

In the following paragraphs, fix the fragments by combining them with the adjoining sentences. Do not add or remove words.

A plump, long-legged spider emerged from the rotten log that I was carrying to the fireplace and fell to the floor. Where it lay on its back for a moment. Before turning clumsily over and making for refuge. Its belly displayed a design in red. Roughly resembling an hour-glass. Recognizing by this danger signal that I was in the presence of a black widow spider. I stepped on the creature.*

I first moved to my present house in 1969. After living in an apartment for over six years. As soon as I moved in I was aware of how much difference there is between living in a rented apartment and a house I owned myself. First of all, there is the matter of upkeep. In an apartment one can always call the owner or a handyman. Who will fix the problem without charge. In a house, on the other hand, everything that needs fixing costs money. Repairmen, electricians, plumbers, and painters, for example. All charge me for their services. There is no landlord to take care of the bill.

The amount of time spent studying for an examination is no sure guarantee of success. My friend Harry is always studying, but no matter how hard he tries. He is never able to do as well as he wants. Another friend, Sheila, never seems to open a book. Yet does well in all her subjects. The answer is not that Harry is dumb and Sheila brilliant. For they are both equally intelligent. The truth is, there are good ways to study and bad ways to study. The study habits and methods themselves make an enormous difference.

EXERCISE 7

Take the following dependent clauses and turn them into complete sentences two different ways. First add words to the ending; then add words to the beginning. In both cases, the words you add will themselves be complete sentences.

1. When I was in sixth grade, _____ .

   _____

   when I was in sixth grade.

2. If the tennis court is dry, _____ .

   _____

   if the tennis court is dry.

3. After the bus driver fainted, _____ .

   _____

   after the bus driver fainted.

*From Berton Roueché, *Eleven Blue Men* (Boston, Mass.: Little, Brown and Company), p. 89.

4. Since the paint is still wet, _____.

_____

since the paint is still wet.

5. Because all her evening shoes were still lying unopened in the green trunk upstairs, _____.

_____

because all her evening shoes were still lying unopened in the green trunk upstairs.

6. That I liked her _____.

_____

that I liked her.

7. Because he used to practice pool for hours, _____.

_____

_____

because he used to practice pool for hours.

8. Since the final is more than two months away, _____.

_____

since the final is more than two months away.

9. While the turkey is in the oven, _____.

_____

while the turkey is in the oven.

10. When they were hanging around the corner drugstore, _____

_____

_____

_____ when they were hanging around the corner drugstore.

Summary
1. A *sentence* has a *subject* and a *verb*.
2. A *verb* shows time.
3. A *subject* answers the question Who? or What? in front of the verb. It can be a *noun*, a *pronoun*, or a *phrase* acting as a noun.
4. A *dependent clause* looks like a sentence, but it has a word in front of it that forces you to connect the clause to a complete sentence.
5. A *fragment* results from
   A. No verb, or
   B. No noun, or
   C. A dependent clause in place of a sentence.

EXERCISE 8

Go back to Exercise 4. You have already picked out the fragments. Now rewrite them, making them into complete sentences. Do the rewriting in the space provided:

1. _____

   _____

2. (correct)

3. _____

   _____

4. _____

   _____

5. _____

   _____

6. _____

   _____

7. (correct)

8. _____

   _____

9. _____

   _____

10. _____

    _____

Run-on Sentences

A run-on is two complete sentences pushed into one:

1. We went home we ate dinner.
2. Luis runs well he won the medal last summer for the hundred-yard dash.
3. Math requires concentration I need to apply myself in order to do well at it.

These run-ons need to be fixed. They have to be separated, for pushing two sentences together—creating a run-on—is an error.

Periods and Semicolons

The easiest way to separate run-ons is to put a period at the end of the first sentence and begin the next one with a capital letter. The first sentence would look like this:

1. *We went home. We ate dinner.*
Fix the next two:

2. _____

_____

3. _____

_____

Some people might be tempted to put a comma between the two sentences, but a comma will not solve the problem. A comma by itself cannot separate complete sentences. There is, however, another mark of punctuation that can sometimes be used instead of the period, the semicolon (;). The semicolon is usually used between two closely related sentences; many times it serves the same function as the word "and." (This last sentence used a semicolon correctly.) When using a semicolon, do not capitalize the first letter of the next word.

Examples

RUN-ON   The store finally ran a sale we arrived early Monday morning.
RUN-ON   The store finally ran a sale, we arrived early Monday morning.
GOOD   The store finally ran a sale. We arrived early Monday morning.
GOOD   The store finally ran a sale; we arrived early Monday morning.

RUN-ON   Gloria hated the movie she never could understand why people liked Westerns.
RUN-ON   Gloria hated the movie, she never could understand why people liked Westerns.
GOOD   Gloria hated the movie. She never could understand why people liked Westerns.
GOOD   Gloria hated the movie; she never could understand why people liked Westerns.

Notice how a period or a semicolon are equally good, but a comma does nothing to fix the run-ons.

EXERCISE 9

Find the run-ons and fix them with a period or a semicolon. Remember to capitalize when necessary.

1. The old house stood alone against the sky it had been empty for years.
2. Every afternoon Mr. Darcey would walk his dog he really loved that poodle.
3. Harry lay very still for a long time then he got up slowly.
4. She hated working in the store all the customers got on her nerves.
5. The lawn seemed endless we couldn't decide how many acres of grass we had mowed.
6. She took the examination ten times finally, when they stopped discriminating, she passed.
7. The office had a tiny desk, a chair, and a two-drawer file cabinet it was all he could afford.
8. Both cats sat in the sunlight mine was asleep.
9. The shopping cart soon filled up a sale like that comes along only once a year.
10. Mile after mile of open road lay ahead Juliet was excited by the possibilities that awaited her.

Commas and Conjunctions

Another way to correct a run-on is to link the separate sentences with a comma plus a conjunction like these:

and	but	so	nor
or	for	yet	

In these cases, the comma and conjunction combine the two sentences into one, so there is no need for a capital letter after the conjunction.

Examples

RUN-ON The store finally ran a sale we arrived early Monday morning.

GOOD The store finally ran a sale, *so* we arrived early Monday morning.

RUN-ON Gloria hated the movie she never could understand why people liked Westerns.

GOOD Gloria hated the movie, *for* she never could understand why people liked Westerns.

EXERCISE 10

Correct these run-ons by adding a comma plus a conjunction.

1. Officers used to insist upon separate living quarters now they don't.
2. The car ran for 100,000 miles its engine needed very little maintenance.
3. Fancy clothes are going out of style they're being replaced by more casual attire.

4. A panel discussion rarely settles issues it can be useful for defining the right kind of question.
5. The plane circled the field for hours then it landed.
6. The water looked tantalizingly close it was still seven miles away.
7. Typing takes more time and trouble the result is usually better than handwriting.
8. He seemed fated to become a fisherman his father and grandfather had been fishermen too.
9. She couldn't decide whether to major in botany or zoology she saw a counselor.
10. One of us has to win it better be me.

(For additional work on conjunctions, see Chapter 5, "Sentence Combining," Exercises 3 and 4.)

TROUBLESOME WORDS

Words like "however," "therefore," "still," "then," "nevertheless," "for example," "for instance," and "in addition" cannot connect sentences grammatically. They must be treated just like any other words when correcting run-ons.

Examples

RUN-ON	I woke up late however I made the bus just in time.
RUN-ON	I woke up late, however, I made the bus just in time.
GOOD	I woke up late. However, I made the bus just in time.
GOOD	I woke up late; however, I made the bus just in time.

These troublesome words often call for a semicolon in front of them and a comma after them.

EXERCISE 11

Fix the run-ons by adding a semicolon.
1. A new car is not necessarily a better car still, there is an immense amount of satisfaction in owning one.
2. I really do not understand the calculus, however, I must admit that I haven't studied it very hard yet.
3. Experienced female employees do not earn as much as similarly qualified males, therefore, on the face of it there is serious inequality.
4. He said that he could not lend me any money, instead, he told me the name of the local finance company.
5. The scientists could not prove the existence of ESP, nevertheless, they were convinced that they should keep looking.

6. Harry was sure he could fix the clock however, he just never got it back together.
7. Sending letters to movie stars was his hobby in addition, he'd keep scrapbooks of pictures from fan magazines.
8. Twenty miles was too much of a hike for beginners nevertheless, Aunt Emily did surprisingly well.
9. We all found the notebook at the same time then we took it immediately to the lost-and-found office.
10. Looks aren't everything for instance, George isn't handsome but his kindness attracts plenty of girls.

(For additional work, see Chapter 5, Exercises 5 and 6.)

Summary

Run-ons occur when two sentences are written as one. Fix them in the following ways:
1. Put a period between the sentences (use a capital).
2. Put a semicolon between the sentences if they are closely related (no capital).
3. Put a comma and conjunction between the sentences (no capital).

EXERCISE 12

Correct the run-ons by adding a period (and a capital), or a semicolon (no capital), or a comma and a conjunction (no capital). Remember that a comma alone will not do the job. Do not take out any words.

1. Every company demands certain things from its employees this one insists that they do a full day's work.
2. My bedroom's walls are very uneven they form odd angles which make hanging wallpaper a difficult task.
3. Alaska is usually terribly cold, however, it's one of the most beautiful places I've ever seen.
4. My neighbor talks about me behind my back, then, when she sees me on the street, she puts on a big smile and gives me a friendly greeting.
5. My block is in a low crime area the trouble we have we create ourselves.
6. In order to study well students must be able to concentrate for example, it's hard to pay attention while the television is going full blast.
7. He left the pastry shop early then at noon he took the ferry to San Francisco.
8. There were some cars in the parking lot one of them was mine.
9. Arranging a surprise party is hard you have to remember that people can unthinkingly give the secret away to the guest of honor.
10. Baseball isn't for me I prefer football.

EXERCISE 13

Correct the run-ons, but do not remove any words.
1. Earning lots of money isn't important using it well is.
2. Skiing is expensive and tiring also, if you're not careful, it can be dangerous.
3. Cats are stubborn they simply will not listen to reason.
4. Marie's sister had a party all her friends came and brought presents.
5. I was born in Georgia it is a lovely state, full of thick forests and rolling hills.
6. I opened the door quietly and crept up the stairs, however, my brother had awakened and was waiting for me as I entered the room.
7. He swung the hammer carelessly and hit his hand it hurt.
8. Mark joined the Navy in order to become an aviator they made him a frogman.
9. The angry woman demanded her money back in addition she insisted upon a written apology.
10. The room had few furnishings there were only a broken-down sofa and a battered coffee table.

Pronoun Reference

Pronouns substitute for nouns, and they must agree with the nouns they refer back to. On most occasions, pronoun reference is clear enough:

I went to *my* bank yesterday.

The two pronouns "I" and "my" refer back to the speaker, the one who went to the bank.

Sally went to *her* bank yesterday.

Here the pronoun "her" refers back to "Sally." These pronouns all have obvious references; it would be hard to get them wrong. But problems do arise with pronouns and the words they refer to, particularly in the areas of *person, number,* and *gender.* Let's look at how mistakes can occur.

PERSON

It is helpful to think of three different forms of person in English:

first person: the <u>speaker</u>   I, my, me, we
second person: the <u>one spoken to</u>   you, your
third person: the <u>one spoken about</u>   he, she, it, they

A novel in which the leading character uses "I" all the time is told in the first person. If the character is called "he" or "she," the tale is told in the third person.

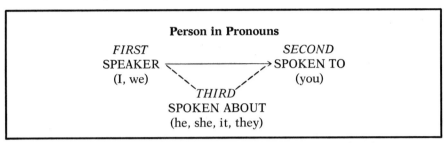

Nouns, whenever they appear, are almost always third person, so any pronoun that replaces them has to be third person also. One common problem is to switch persons in the middle of a sentence:

1. When <u>someone</u> needs a new phonograph needle, <u>you</u> can go to the hi-fi store and buy a replacement for about ten dollars.

"Someone" is third person, but the pronoun that refers back to it is second person, "you." "Someone" can only be replaced by another third person pronoun, not by a second person pronoun like "you." (Use "he" or "she.")

2. As <u>one</u> enters the forest, <u>you</u> find <u>yourself</u> surrounded by the tallest redwoods in California.

The word "one" absolutely demands another third person pronoun to replace it, but here the second person "you" has crept in.

Both sentences can be rewritten in two different ways.

Rewritten Versions

1(a). When <u>someone</u> needs a new phonograph needle, <u>he</u> or <u>she</u> can go to the hi-fi store and buy a replacement for about ten dollars. (third person)

1(b). When <u>you</u> need a new phonograph needle, <u>you</u> can go to the hi-fi store and buy a replacement for about ten dollars. (second person)

2(a). As <u>one</u> enters the forest, <u>one</u> finds <u>oneself</u> surrounded by the tallest redwoods in California. (third person)

2(b). As <u>you</u> enter the forest, <u>you</u> find <u>yourself</u> surrounded by the tallest redwoods in California. (second person)

In both cases the pronouns had to be changed to make them refer to each other clearly.

You probably noticed that 1(a) and 2(a) sounded more formal than 1(b) and 2(b). The difference comes from the use of the word "you," a mark of the informal style. The more formal the essay, the fewer times the word "you" will appear. And whenever you write, be careful not to switch to "you" when your sentence has committed you to using a third person pronoun like "he," "she," "one," or "they."

EXERCISE 14

The following sentences need to be rewritten to clear up errors of pronoun reference. Don't change the underlined noun or pronoun.

1. When <u>someone</u> visits Mexico, you usually buy more souvenirs than you know what to do with.

   _____

   _____

2. A football <u>player</u> needs to practice for long hours, but you should save some energy for when you are in the game.

   _____

   _____

3. A <u>person</u> may pass the written part of the driver's test, but until you're behind the wheel you'll never know how well you'll handle a car.

   _____

   _____

4. A <u>thief</u> can steal thousands of dollars, but you can also wind up spending years in jail.

   _____

   _____

5. If a <u>couple</u> plans to get married, the two of you should decide in advance whether or not you want children.

   _____

   _____

6. Many <u>Americans</u> have their television sets on for seven hours a day, but that doesn't mean that you are watching attentively; instead the sets may be used as "background" while you do other tasks about the house.

   _____

   _____

7. All new <u>freshmen</u> must bring high school grades and placement tests to the admissions office when you register.

   _____

   _____

8. When a large <u>group</u> of people arrived for dinner, the restaurant used to put you all in a separate dining room.

_____

_____

9. <u>People</u> who feel they have been the victims of discrimination should complain to the proper government agency; it's also a good idea for you to engage a lawyer as well.

_____

_____

10. He treated his <u>guests</u> courteously enough, but you sometimes got the feeling that he wasn't really glad to see you.

_____

_____

A SPECIAL CASE OF PERSON—THE "FLOATING" _THEY_

In _conversation_ we often say sentences like:

1. They ought to fix these potholes.
2. Why can't they get a better shortstop?
3. I wish they would make the aisles wider.
4. How do they want us to fill out this form?
5. Why don't they have a law against that?

Writing demands that the sentences be more specific; readers have to be told very clearly who "they" are. Good style in writing would mean certain changes:

1. The _highway department_ ought to fix these potholes.
2. Why can't _the Cubs_ get a better shortstop?

EXERCISE 15

Rewrite the next three in the list above.

3. _____

4. _____

5. _____

It is not necessary to indicate who "they" are in _every_ sentence of a paragraph; all you need is one clear indication at the beginning. But never use a "they" without a clear, explicit connection that the reader can easily find.

EXERCISE 16

Add a clear indication of who "they" are to the following groups of sentences. (Sometimes you'll find that you can replace the "they" with another word that will do the job more efficiently.) The first two are done for you:

1. Daytona is my favorite beach. *They* have miles of clean sand, perfect weather, and the best breakers on the Florida coast.

Rewrite: Daytona is my favorite beach. It has miles of clean sand, perfect weather, and the best breakers on the Florida coast.

2. The waterfront bar was a hostile place. *They* looked us over and made us feel as if we were intruding.

Rewrite: The people in the waterfront bar were hostile. They looked us over and made us feel as if we were intruding.

or: The waterfront bar was a hostile place. The people there looked us over and made us feel as if we were intruding.

Notice that there is always more than one solution; all you need to do is make clear who or what you mean. Now rewrite the following sentences.

3. In my dormitory they have a lounge that is open all night.

_____

_____

4. In such a big supermarket they ought to have better signs to guide the customers.

_____

_____

5. Caliban County College has enrolled thousands of new students because they offer courses that can't be found elsewhere.

_____

_____

6. Imported cameras have such a large share of the market because they manufacture them abroad, where they don't have to pay their employees high American wages.

_____

_____

7. The Republican Party may be losing membership, but they still have managed to get their presidential candidates elected frequently.

_____

_____

8. The drug problem could be reduced if only they would change the laws and enforce them more fairly.

_____

_____

9. In Kansas they had a law against serving drinks in restaurants and bars.

_____

_____

10. On my last flight they served ham sandwiches that tasted like plastic.

_____

_____

GENDER

The word _gender_ refers to whether the word is masculine, feminine, or neuter. In English the distinctions are simple: all males are masculine, all females are feminine, and everything else is neuter. There are a few exceptions, notably ships and planes, which often are considered feminine ("She's a good ship.") and infants and animals, which are often referred to as neuter ("It's a beautiful baby." "What's its name?")

The gender of pronouns would be a simple matter to decide if there were not words that could refer to _both_ males and females. Look at this sentence:

Every student must report to _____ adviser.

Which pronoun should go in, "his," "her," or "his or her"? The traditional way of writing such sentences was to use "his," which was considered a "neutral" word to refer back to a word that was masculine or feminine. But, of course, "his" is not exactly neutral; it is specifically masculine, and women complain that they're being discriminated against by English grammar. The choices are:

1. Every student must report to <u>his</u> adviser.
   (The traditional solution)
2. Every student must report to <u>his or her</u> adviser.
   (An awkward compromise)

3. <u>All</u> student<u>s</u> must report to <u>their</u> advisers.
(Avoids the problem by putting the sentence into the plural, for "they" and "their" are both masculine and feminine)

The best solution is clearly the third one; the meaning stays the same and the clarity is preserved, along with feelings and good style.

NUMBER

The word *number* refers to whether the pronoun is singular or plural. A pronoun that refers back to a singular noun must be singular; if it refers to a plural noun, it must be plural:

Examples
1. The <u>car</u> lost <u>its</u> headlights, so <u>it</u> cannot be driven after dark.
"Car" is singular, so it must be replaced by a singular pronoun. Since it is neuter, the right pronoun is "it."
2. The <u>cars</u> lost <u>their</u> headlights, so <u>they</u> cannot be driven after dark.
"Cars" is plural, so it must be replaced by a plural pronoun, "they."

There are some pronouns that look as though they are plural, but require the singular nonetheless:

Everyone	Everybody	Everything
Anyone	Anybody	Anything

They all take singular verbs:

Everybody <u>is</u> here. <u>Is</u> anybody home? Let's hope everything <u>goes</u> well.

When it comes to referring back to these words, there are opportunities for choice. Look at the following sentences:

1. Everybody is taking _____ shoes off.
2. Did somebody lose _____ pen?

What should fit into those blanks?

The traditional answer is that, since the words "everybody" and "somebody" are singular and take singular verbs, the words that refer back to them must be singular as well. Thus, the only possible answers to a traditionalist would be:

1. Everybody is taking <u>his</u> shoes off.
2. Did somebody lose <u>his</u> pen?

Here, the "neutral" word "his" serves as the replacement.

Formal writing today still insists upon the traditional distinction. If you are writing a very formal paper, use the "his" just as in the sentences above.

The normal way of *speaking* such sentences is influencing the way they are written. Most people would probably *say*:

1. Everybody is taking <u>their</u> shoes off.
2. Did somebody lose <u>their</u> pen?

Because the "his" is evidence of discrimination to some women, and because speaking employs the informal "their," writing is moving slowly toward dropping the "his" and using the "their." But the matter is not settled yet, and will not be for a long time. Perhaps the safest course would be to put such sentences in the plural:

1. The <u>people</u> are taking off <u>their</u> shoes.

or, to leave out the offending pronoun:

2. Did somebody lose <u>a</u> pen?

EXERCISE 17

Underline the correct word in the following sentences. In some of them you can make a case for both words; which ones?
1. All of the players want to do his/their best.
2. Each one want/wants to do his/their/her best.
3. Is/are everyone satisfied with his/her/their lunch?
4. Neither of the sisters look/looks like her/their mother.
5. Every scorecard was/were turned in with its/their covers wet from the rain.
6. Once some people start taking drugs, they aren't able to stop using it/them.
7. The women who live/lives alone has/have asked the telephone company to give them/her unlisted numbers.
8. Bread fresh from the oven tastes better than it/they do/does when cooled off.
9. Radio isn't as good as it once was; they/it never has/have as many interesting programs as before.
10. When the government wants to build a highway, it/they just forces you to sell it/them your house and land.

CLARITY IN PRONOUN REFERENCE

A pronoun must not only agree with the word it replaces; there must also be no doubt about what that word is. Look at these sentences:

1. Because the frame of my bicycle got bent, I had to replace it. (replace what? the frame? the bicycle?)
2. My car blew its engine, so I had to buy a new one. (new car? new engine?)
3. When Sally moved to Chicago, she was astounded at how busy they all were. (who does the "they" refer to? We know vaguely, but it needs to be clear.)

Every one of the sentences above is unclear. All must be rewritten to make the references unmistakable.

Rewrite

(1) I had to replace the bent frame on my bicycle.
(2) I had to buy a new car because the old one's engine blew.
(3) When Sally moved to Chicago, she was astounded at how busy everyone was.

The words that cause the most vagueness are:

it	that
this	which

Make sure that these pronouns refer back clearly to a noun. The following sentences do not have such a noun (called an "antecedent") and are examples of unclear pronoun reference:

4. The pilot was drunk, which made the passengers nervous. (What <u>noun</u> does "which" refer to? None.)
5. The pilot was drunk, and it made the passengers nervous. (What <u>noun</u> does "it" refer to? None.)
6. The pilot was drunk. This made the passengers nervous. (What <u>noun</u> does "this" refer to? None.)

Rewrite

(4) It made the passengers nervous to see that the pilot was drunk.
Or
(5) The passengers became nervous when they saw that the pilot was drunk.
Or
(6) The drunken pilot made the passengers nervous.

Clear pronoun reference is not just a fine point of style; it is one of the fundamental marks of good prose. Be particularly careful about tacking on phrases and dependent clauses beginning with "which" to the end of sentences. Also watch out for using "this" when it does not refer to a noun or a clearly stated idea.

EXERCISE 18

Rewrite the following sentences, eliminating problems of clear pronoun reference. Many need thorough revision.
Example
  He spent the day in a museum, and this made him understand more about the history of modern painting.
Rewritten
  His day in the museum made him understand more about the history of modern painting.
1. I always avoid walking under ladders, which means bad luck.

_____

_____

2. Arlene loved Tom, which made Frank very jealous.

_____

_____

3. They camped by the river, which was what they planned to do before
they arrived.

_____

_____

4. It says that freshmen cannot use the parking lots, and I think this is
ridiculous.

_____

_____

5. Our old ladder was badly weathered, and this made the carpenter
urge us to buy a new one.

_____

_____

Switching Person in Paragraphs

In paragraphs, make sure you keep to the same person. Never switch from
"he" to "you" to "I" when you move from sentence to sentence. The entire
paragraph must have a consistent point of view.

EXERCISE 19

Rewrite the following sentences in order to clarify the pronoun references.

1. The airport was so big that they had to install a train line to connect
the different terminal buildings.

_____

_____

2. When everyone arrives at the station, be sure to claim all your
luggage from the porter.

_____

_____

3. We all went to a restaurant where they made you wear a jacket and
tie for dinner.

_____

_____

4. I live in New York, which just happens to be the largest city in the whole country.

_____

_____

5. They don't allow parking downtown, and this is very inconvenient when you want to go shopping.

_____

_____

6. I don't go to movies that try to scare you to death.

_____

7. Does everybody have their ticket?

_____

8. When someone looks for a pet, they go to the local animal shelter, and this is a good idea.

_____

_____

9. In Texas they make you feel at home.

_____

10. The shoes they sell these days always hurt your feet.

_____

Improving Sentence Style

Two important elements of good sentence style are parallel structure and related phrases. These terms both stem from one simple rule: Individual parts must clearly refer to the meaning of the whole sentence.

Let's look at the two parts to this rule.

PARALLEL STRUCTURE

Within a sentence, similar things should be written in similar ways.

1. During her vacation she went swimming, fishing, sailing, and she climbed mountains.

This is faulty parallelism. Her actions were:

swimm<u>ing</u>
fish<u>ing</u>
sail<u>ing</u>
clim<u>bed</u> mountains

The problem is obviously with "climbed mountains." The other activities are all listed in similar form; that is, all end in "-ing." But *everything* needs to be listed that way to preserve the parallel structure. Here, "mountain climb<u>ing</u>" or even "climb<u>ing</u>" would have been good parallelism. The improved version of the sentence would now read:

1(a). During her vacation she went swimm<u>ing</u>, fish<u>ing</u>, sail<u>ing</u>, and mountain climb<u>ing</u>.

or

1(b). During her vacation she <u>swam</u>, fish<u>ed</u>, sail<u>ed</u>, and clim<u>bed</u> mountains.

See if you can tell where the parallel breaks down in this example:

2. Two of his favorite methods for becoming a better artist were to paint
watercolors of people and drawing sketches of buildings.

The faulty parallel is caused by the way the two different activities are presented:

... <u>to paint</u> watercolors of people ...
... <u>drawing</u> sketches of buildings.

They should be phrased the same way:

<u>to paint</u> watercolors of people ... and <u>to draw</u> sketches ...
or
<u>painting</u> watercolors of people ... and <u>drawing</u> sketches ...

The repetition of the "-ing" *or* the "to" can help the reader see the connection. Another kind of repetition can also make your parallels clearer. Try repeating the word that introduces the parallel:

3. She judged the paintings *for* accuracy, *for* style, and *for* quality.
4. They all felt *that he had* cheated, *that he had* lied, and *that he
had* been let off lightly.

This is one of the times when repetition can help; it actually points out and emphasizes the structure of what is said.

Some groups of words absolutely demand a parallel construction:

not only ... but also
either ... or
neither ... nor
then ... now
yesterday ... today

both ... and
whether ... or
on one hand ... on the other hand

Examples

1. He insisted that he hated both <u>watching</u> football and <u>to play</u> it. (faulty parallel)
2. He insisted that he hated both <u>watching</u> football and <u>playing</u> it. (good parallel)
3. He insisted that he hated both <u>watching</u> and <u>playing</u> football. (good parallel)
4. She could never decide whether <u>to stay</u> or if she should <u>leave.</u> (faulty parallel)
5. She could never decide whether <u>to stay</u> or <u>to leave.</u> (good parallel)

EXERCISE 20

Rewrite the following sentences by correcting the faulty parallels.

1. The saleswoman was curious, amused, and she helped me.

   _____

2. On the one hand she was thinking of staying home, but on the other she wanted to go out.

   _____

3. The ship's captain acted with daring, bravely, and he showed intelligence.

   _____

4. Their coach knew they had practiced hard and that they were eager to win.

   _____

5. I can't decide whether to get married or if I should stay single.

   _____

6. Since it was her day off, Judge Lewis sat around the house, read the paper, and was thinking of going for a walk.

   _____

7. Steel is important for the automobile industry, for construction work, and also shipbuilding.

   _____

8. Young children like both playing in dirt and to step in deep puddles.

   _____

9. Uncle Frank not only hated washing dishes, but he also never takes out the garbage.

   _____

10. The plane banked sharply, cut its power, and was heading for a steep dive toward the ocean.

   _____

DANGLING PHRASES

A phrase that begins a sentence must be followed immediately by the word that phrase refers to. Look at these examples of what can go wrong when this rule is not applied:

1. After eating dinner, my foot fell asleep.
   (Who ate dinner? Sounds like the foot did.)
2. Walking on the beach, the lighthouse loomed ahead.
   (This says that the lighthouse was walking.)
3. While drinking a can of beer, my television broke.
   (The television drinking beer?)

These are all *dangling phrases*. In each case the opening phrase does not connect with the word it should. In the first sentence the person doing the eating—the owner of the foot—must be mentioned after the comma:

1(a). After eating dinner, I felt my foot fall asleep.

In the second, the person doing the walking should follow the comma:

2(a). Walking on the beach, she saw the lighthouse loom up ahead.

How would you fix the third sentence?

3(a). _____

In the first three examples the dangling phrases have an "-ing" word (called a "present participle") in them. Other constructions can cause the same problem:

4. To finish the job, a new door must be installed. (Dangles. The door will finish the job?)
4(a). To finish the job, install a new door. (Good)
5. Tired of waiting for the bus, a taxi was called. (Dangles. The taxi was waiting for a bus?)
5(a). Tired of waiting for the bus, I called a taxi. (Good)
6. While still hung over, George reminded me of what I did the night before. (Who had the hangover?)

This makes it sound as if George was hung over. If so, fine; if George wasn't the one with the hangover, rewrite the sentence:

6(a). While I was still hung over, George reminded me of what I had done the night before.

EXERCISE 21

Complete the following ten sentences. Begin them with the words given and arrange them so that the first phrases are followed by a comma. Be sure to avoid dangling phrases.

1. Looking _____

   _____ .

2. After being _____

   _____ .

3. While trying _____

   _____ .

4. Sick of _____

   _____ .

5. When walking _____

   _____ .

6. To get _____

   _____ .

7. Worn out with _____

   _____ .

8. To stop _____

   _____ .

9. Expecting _____

   _____ .

10. Tired from _____

   _____ .

WORDINESS

The best writers make every word count. Their sentences may be long or short, but in them every single word makes an impact. One way good writers manage to get the most out of every word is through the process of *revising*. After they have written a sentence, paragraph, or essay, they go through it trying to eliminate unnecessary words. Look at these examples:

The man who is coming to dinner lives in the house that is next door to mine.

There are no problems with the grammar of that sentence, but there are extra words. A good writer would cut it down like this:

The man ~~who is~~ coming to dinner lives ~~in the house that is~~ next door ~~to mine.~~ (The man coming to dinner lives next door.)

All the unnecessary words have been removed, leaving a shorter, cleaner sentence. There are many opportunities to cut down on words. Here are some:

1. When the sentence is too full of "who," "what," "which," and "that," remove them.

Example

A person who was living there would know what he had to do.
(A person living there would know what to do.)
This is the book that I liked.
(This is the book I liked.)

2. When words are repeated unnecessarily, rephrase the sentence:

Example

If you dislike the noise of a great city, city life is not for you.
(If you dislike noise, city life is not for you.)
Potato chips are my favorite snack. They are my favorite snack because they taste salty and crispy.
(Potato chips are my favorite snack because they taste salty and crispy.)

3. Strings of short, simple sentences can often be combined into larger, more complicated sentences:

Example

I switched on the television. I let it warm up. Then I turned to the channel I wanted to watch.
(I switched on the television, let it warm up, then turned to the channel I wanted.)

EXERCISE 22

Rewrite the following, eliminating extra words and combining short sentences into longer ones when necessary. The first one is done for you:

1. The first person that I met at the party was Cindy. Cindy was a blonde who had bright green eyes.

Rewritten: The first person I met at the party was Cindy, a blonde with bright green eyes.

2. The woman who was keeping score made a mistake.

_____

_____

3. The trail that I followed led to a boulder that was perched on the edge of a cliff.

_____

_____

4. Aluminum is a metal that is very light in weight.

_____

_____

5. The office manager wanted all the memos to be typed. She wanted all the memos to be typed so that they would be easy to read.

_____

_____

6. I spent two years in Tucson. Tucson is my favorite city.

_____

_____

7. The license plate that was on the car had a word on it instead of numbers. The word was "rodeo."

_____

_____

8. The book that the library wants me to return is called _For Whom the Bell Tolls_.

_____

_____

9. She flew to Hawaii on a 747. The 747 is the biggest airliner in the world.

_____

_____

10. All the cigars that he smoked made the room smell like it was a tobacco factory.

_____

_____

(For additional exercises see "Sentence Combining," Chapter 5, Exercises 8, 9, 10, and 13.)

MASTERY TEST I FOR SENTENCE SENSE

Correct the following sentences for fragments, run-ons, or poor pronoun reference. If the sentence is correct, put a "C" in the margin.

1. The most spectacular sunset I ever saw.

2. They tried to rescue all three swimmers, unfortunately, only two were saved.

3. A matter of opinion that cannot be settled by proof or evidence.

4. It stopped.

5. She got her exercise from running around the track, swimming in the pool, and she played volleyball.

6. For example, serving mustard with frankfurters.

7. Turning the corner sharply, the next block looked deserted.

8. He soon tired of studying and taking tests then he dropped out of school permanently.

9. Put on the red jacket with the extra long sleeves.

10. Those pickles that come in a little stone crock.

11. Every one of those companies that pay less than the minimum wage.

---

12. All of the players quit early the sun was unbearable.

---

13. Tired of standing in the snow, the station was invaded by the angry commuters.

---

14. Most of the old signposts were from bakers, butchers, and men who made candles.

---

15. Arriving well past 7:00 P.M. on a cold, snowy November night.

MASTERY TEST II FOR SENTENCE SENSE

Correct the following sentences. If the sentence is already correct, write a "C" in the margin.

1. The train always slowed down at the crossing this was because there was no gate or warning sign.

---

2. Early twentieth-century immigrants to America were often greeted by hostility, which was something that surprised them.

---

3. Fixing his eyes on the clock, the announcement that class would end was made by the professor.

---

4. It is not always a simple matter to acquire a good reading style, in fact, it's often impossible.

---

5. They all enjoyed sailing in Chesapeake Bay, canoeing on the Potomac, and to swim at Lake Warner.

_____

_____

6. Acting in the manner that was expected of her.

_____

_____

7. Only after many years of hard work did Carver come up with what are now considered his most important discoveries.

_____

_____

8. Watching television, reading magazines, and to go to the movies are three ways of passing time.

_____

_____

9. The best brand of washing machine the store had in stock.

_____

_____

10. Opinions differ on the usefulness of passenger trains some influential legislators dislike them.

_____

_____

11. Unknown to everyone who was sitting in the crowded theater.

_____

_____

12. The secretary typed the letter, inserted it in the envelope, then she sent it to the mailroom.

_____

_____

13. Authoritative reports agree the weather is getting colder.

_____

_____

14. Turning the corner quickly, the football stadium came into view.

_____

_____

15. Mr. Hudson preferred football, tennis, and to play cricket.

_____

_____

CHAPTER 5

TOWARD MATURE SENTENCES

Sentence Combining

One mark of good writing is sentence variety. When all the sentences follow the same pattern, the reader gets weary and loses interest. Varied sentences, long mixed with short, provide an ever-new interplay of ideas and feelings. They communicate better and serve to mark the writer as knowledgeable and fluent.

This section of the book contains fifteen different ways to make your sentences more interesting. The basic assumption is that the normal sentence pattern needs to be varied by addition. Short sentences become longer and more interesting by adding words, phrases, and sometimes whole sentences. It's important to understand how this can be done. Here are the basic sentence patterns that you will be using:

1. SUBJECT + VERB   She ran.

2. SUBJECT + VERB + conjunction + SUBJECT +   VERB
    She   ran   and   he   followed.

3. SUBJECT + VERB + dependent clause
    She   ran   while he followed.

4. SUBJECT + VERB +   phrase
     She   ran   with him following closely.

5. Dependent clause   + SUBJECT + VERB
    Since he followed,   she   ran.

6.   Phrase   + SUBJECT + VERB
    With him following,   she   ran.

In every one of these six basic patterns, the original sentence remains the same ("She ran"), but it has been made longer by adding words. What had been a short sentence of only a subject and a verb has now become a longer, more varied sentence; it *says* more. The exercises in this section will help you to say more in your own sentences, using these patterns and other more complex ones as well.

ADDING DESCRIPTIVE WORDS

One way to make your sentences sharper and more detailed is to place descriptive words (adjectives) in front of nouns.

Example
(a) The problem required a solution.
(b) The problem was knotty.
(c) The solution had to be immediate.
COMBINED: The knotty problem required an immediate solution.

The descriptive words have been moved from sentences (b) and (c) into the main sentence (a). Do the same to the sentences in Exercise 1.

EXERCISE 1

1. (a) A breeze floated in from the ocean.
   (b) The breeze was humid.
   (c) The ocean was calm.

COMBINED: _____

_____

2. (a) Some convicts escaped from the prison.
   (b) There were thirteen convicts.
   (c) The convicts were dangerous.
   (d) It was a maximum-security prison.

COMBINED: _____

3. (a) All her energy was concentrated on her job.
    (b) Her energy was enormous.
    (c) Her job was demanding.

COMBINED: _____

_____

4. (a) Grimaldi's advice impressed the politicians.
    (b) The advice was realistic.
    (c) The politicians were inexperienced.

COMBINED: _____

5. Supply two sentences with descriptive words and then combine them.
    (a) The day began with breakfast.

    (b) _____

    (c) _____

COMBINED: _____

_____

EXERCISE 2

Write the following five sets. First write a main sentence, then two sentences containing descriptive words, and finally combine all three.

1. (a) _____

    _____

    (b) _____

    (c) _____

COMBINED: _____

_____

2. (a) _____

    _____

    (b) _____

    (c) _____

COMBINED: _____

_____

3. (a) _____

_____

(b) _____

(c) _____

COMBINED: _____

_____

4. (a) _____

_____

(b) _____

(c) _____

COMBINED: _____

_____

5. (a) _____

_____

(b) _____

(c) _____

COMBINED: _____

_____

LINKING SENTENCES TOGETHER

One of the easiest ways to combine sentences is to link them together by means of the following words:

and	or	so	nor
but	for	yet	

These words (conjunctions) can join together two or even three sentences, as in the following example:

Example
(a) The film ended at eleven.
(b) We did not arrive home until midnight.
COMBINED: The film ended at eleven, *but* we did not arrive home until midnight.
(The word *yet* could be used in place of *but*. Could *so*? Would *and* make the connection stronger or weaker?)

EXERCISE 3

In the following sentences, insert a comma and one of the words listed on page 127 (of course you will have to remove the period and the capital letter too).

1. (a) Alexander Hamilton was born in the West Indies.
   (b) Hamilton spent most of his life in New York.
   (Be sure to replace *Hamilton* with *he* when you join these.)

COMBINED: _____

2. (a) I could not see any pedestrians.
   (b) I drove through the intersection.

COMBINED: _____

3. (a) He may be dumb.
   (b) He is still dangerous.

COMBINED: _____

4. (a) She walked around the office making sure everything was locked up.
   (b) Then she turned off the light and closed the door.

COMBINED: _____

5. (a) The trail lay buried under a thick blanket of snow.
   (b) The tracker could still follow it perfectly.

COMBINED: _____

_____

EXERCISE 4

In each of the following sets, make up the second sentence yourself and then combine it with the first by means of a conjunction:

1. (a) Friday was usually her hardest day at the office.

   (b) _____

   _____

COMBINED: _____

_____

2. (a) The first stop on the journey turned out to be Chicago.

(b) _____

_____

COMBINED: _____

_____

3. (a) The old houses sat in a long, gloomy row.

(b) _____

_____

COMBINED: _____

_____

4. Now make up all three parts: an original sentence (a), the key sentence (b), and the combined sentence that joins (a) and (b) by means of a conjunction.

(a) _____

_____

(b) _____

_____

COMBINED: _____

_____

5. (a) _____

_____

(b) _____

_____

COMBINED: _____

_____

Note: Compare these sentence combinations with the run-on sentences in Chapter 4, pages 99–104.

USING SEMICOLONS

You can combine sentences by using the semicolon (;) and one of the following words:

However	Furthermore	On the other hand
Therefore	Still	
Moreover	Nevertheless	In addition

Remember: **A** semicolon can be used only between two grammatically complete sentences. (It is never followed by a capital.) The words listed above *cannot* connect two sentences; the semicolon does the combining.

Example
(a) We left them all behind. (; however,)
(b) They were not forgotten.
COMBINED: We left them all behind; however, they were not forgotten.
(Notice that *nevertheless* could be substituted for *however*. Could *therefore*? How about *still*?)

EXERCISE 5

INSTRUCTIONS: After sentence (a) add a semicolon; then use one of the words listed above, and a comma. Then add sentence (b) *without* using a capital letter.

1. (a) The soil in Bordeaux has little else in it but clay and chalk.
    (b) It grows the world's best grapes.

COMBINED: _____

---

2. (a) In the seventeenth century Holland was a tiny nation of merchants and seamen.
    (b) The Dutch built up a great commercial empire in a few short generations.

COMBINED: _____

---

3. (a) Astronomers speculate that somewhere among the countless billion stars there must be intelligent life.
    (b) So far signs of such life are entirely lacking.

COMBINED: _____

---

4. (a) By 7 P.M. the temperature on the field registered thirty-five degrees.
    (b) The commissioner decided to go ahead with the game.

COMBINED: _____

5. (a) She was the studio's best actress.
   (b) She never became a star.

COMBINED: _____

_____

EXERCISE 6

Now make up the second sentence yourself and combine it with (a), the
one provided.

1. (a) The play was a sellout.

   (b) _____

COMBINED: _____

2. (a) Not one speaker hinted at the problem.

   (b) _____

COMBINED: _____

3. (a) A purebred dog costs up to five hundred dollars.

   (b) _____

COMBINED: _____

Now make up all three sentences, combining them with a semicolon,
one of the words listed at the top of page 130, and a comma.

4. (a) _____

   (b) _____

COMBINED: _____

5. (a) _____

   (b) _____

COMBINED: _____

Note: Turn to "Run-on Sentences" (pages 100–104) for more work with
semicolons.

WRITING LONGER SENTENCES

You can combine three sentences into one by means of commas and by crossing out words that are repeated.

Example
(a) The engine coughed.
(b) The engine sputtered.
(c) Then the engine quit altogether.
COMBINED: The engine coughed, sputtered, then quit altogether.

Notice that the words "the engine" in (b) and (c) were dropped. If they were not eliminated, a run-on sentence would result (The engine coughed, the engine sputtered.).

Example
(a) Alan opened the book/,
(b) ~~Alan~~ took notes for five minutes/,
(c) Then ~~Alan~~ returned it to the shelf.
COMBINED: Alan opened the book, took notes for five minutes, then returned
it to the shelf.

EXERCISE 7

Remove all repetitious words and combine.
1. (a) Alice opened the door.
   (b) Alice turned on the light.
   (c) Then Alice recoiled in horror at the body on the garage floor.

COMBINED: _____

---

2. (a) The dog pawed the ground nervously.
   (b) The dog growled fiercely.
   (c) Then the dog launched itself straight at the letter carrier's
       ankle.

COMBINED: _____

---

3. (a) The bugle's sound pierced the stillness.
   (b) The sound echoed from the distant shore.
   (c) Then the sound reverberated dimly in the crisp Arctic air.

COMBINED: _____

---

4. (a) The doctor considered her options.
   (b) The doctor made her decision.
   (c) Then the doctor strode to the phone and dialed the hospital.

COMBINED: _____

---

5. (a) The driver raced the engine.
   (b) The driver released the clutch.
   (c) The driver peeled out with an earsplitting screech.

COMBINED: _____

---

6. (a) The agent sized up the situation instantly.
   (b) The agent boarded the train.
   (c) The agent sat down inconspicuously in the smoking compart-
   ment.

COMBINED: _____

Now write one of your own sentences, the third, before you combine.
7. (a) The train rang its bell.
   (b) The train blew its whistle.

   (c) _____

COMBINED: _____

---

8. (a) Last Saturday morning I did all our shopping.
   (b) I vacuumed the living room.

   (c) _____

COMBINED: _____

Now make up a whole series of your own.

9. (a) _____

   (b) _____

   (c) _____

COMBINED: _____

---

10. (a) _____

    (b) _____

    (c) _____

COMBINED: _____

ADDING CONNECTING WORDS

You can use connecting words to combine short sentences into longer, more detailed ones. Study this list of the most common connecting words:

after	before	unless
although	how	until
as	if	when
because	since	while

(Remember that these words can connect when they are in combinations as well: just before, long after, whenever, as if.)

Example

(a) He finished his years in the army. (AFTER . . .)
(b) He became an acrobat with the circus.
COMBINED: After he finished his years in the army, he became an acrobat with the circus.
Could another connecting word do the job of linking the two sentences? Which one?

EXERCISE 8

INSTRUCTIONS: Place the connecting word in front of sentence (b).
Put sentence (b) (with the connecting word) in front.
Insert a comma.
Change the capital letter in (a) if necessary.
When you have finished, the result will be one sentence where two existed before.

1. (a) The state built two new throughways through the nature reserve. (SINCE . . .)
    (b) All the wildlife disappeared.

COMBINED: _____

---

2. (a) Mayor Wigglesworth favored the proposal. (ALTHOUGH . . .)
    (b) Pressure from the lobbyists finally won out.

COMBINED: _____

---

3. (a) You are going to see Ellen. (IF . . .)
    (b) Tell her I miss her.

COMBINED: _____

---

4. (a) Your reasoning seems good. (WHILE . . .)
    (b) I cannot agree with your conclusion.

COMBINED: _____

---

5. (a) Mobile homes are mass-produced in a factory and shipped to a building site. (SINCE . . .)
    (b) They provide a cheap alternative to conventional housing.

COMBINED: _____

_____

6. (a) The job paid her barely enough to live on. (ALTHOUGH . . .)
    (b) Alice loved working at the hospital.

COMBINED: _____

_____

Now try putting the connecting word and sentence (b) *in the middle* of the long sentence (no comma needed here).

7. (a) A light bulb burned out. (WHENEVER . . .)
    (b) Uncle Elmer suspected that the electric company was trying to cheat him.

COMBINED: Whenever _____

_____

COMBINED: _____ whenever _____

_____

8. (a) Dinner time came around. (JUST BEFORE . . .)
    (b) The mutt displayed his best behavior.

COMBINED: Just before _____

_____

COMBINED: _____ just before _____

_____

9. (a) The concert ended in a shower of boos and hisses. (RIGHT AF-TER . . .)
    (b) The conductor handed in his resignation.

COMBINED: _____ right after _____

_____

COMBINED: Right after _____

_____

10. (a) I understand what the jury's verdict is. (UNTIL . . .)
    (b) Tell the crowd that they will have to wait.

COMBINED: _____ until _____

_____

COMBINED: Until _____

_____

Note: Review "Sentences and Fragments" (pages 90–98) to refresh your memory of the special problems caused by misuse of connecting words.

DROPPING UNNECESSARY WORDS

You can combine two sentences by making the second one part of the first and dropping unnecessary words.

Example
(a) My street never has any traffic.
(b) The reason my street never has traffic is because the pavement is full of potholes.
COMBINED: My street never has any traffic because the pavement is full of potholes.

EXERCISE 9

Complete the following combinations.

1. (a) Shopping centers have proved to be tremendously popular.
   (b) They are popular because they offer variety, easy access, and free parking.

COMBINED: _____

---

2. (a) My father never gave me an allowance.
   (b) He never gave me an allowance because he thought I should earn my own money.

COMBINED: _____

---

3. (a) It is illegal to import leopard skins.
   (b) This is because the government wants to protect leopards, an endangered species, from hunters.

COMBINED: _____

---

4. (a) My favorite month is October.
   (b) October is when the air is crisp and the leaves turn to brilliant reds and oranges.

COMBINED: _____

---

5. (a) The judge sentenced her to three years.
   (b) The sentence was so long on account of her unrepentant attitude.

COMBINED: _____

---

6. (a) It is always best to take time to consider the type of house you want.
   (b) The type of house is important because if you are not satisfied with the style, you probably will not enjoy living there, no matter how pleasant the neighborhood may be.

COMBINED: _____

_____

7. (a) Her alimony check was late again.
   (b) Because of this, she called her lawyer.

COMBINED: _____

8. (a) Gabriel Fahrenheit (1686–1736) was an early experimenter in measuring heat and cold.
   (b) Because of this, a thermometer scale was named after him.

COMBINED: _____

9. (a) I arrived late to work today.
   (b) I was late because I forgot to set my alarm clock.

COMBINED: _____

10. (a) Objects like old catalogues, faded postcards, and clothing from thirty years ago were recently thought worthless but are now bringing in high prices.
    (b) The prices are high because such items are now in demand as antiques.

COMBINED: _____

_____

_____

MAKING INTRODUCTORY PHRASES

When you have two sentences you want to combine, you can add or drop words and phrases from the second to make it an introductory phrase of the first. The introductory phrase is separated from the rest of the new sentence by a comma.

Example

(a) The secretary demanded an enormous raise.
(b) The secretary was *determined to be aggressive*.
COMBINED: Determined to be aggressive, the secretary demanded an enormous raise.

EXERCISE 10

As you can see from the example, part of sentence (b) should be put in front of sentence (a).

1. (a) My father went downstairs to check for burglars.
   (b) My father was *alarmed by the unfamiliar sound*.(,)

COMBINED: ―――――――――――――――――――――――――

2. (a) Franklin started negotiating on his own.
   (b) Franklin had grown *tired of waiting for instructions from Washington*.(,)

COMBINED: ―――――――――――――――――――――――――

3. (a) The President doodled in her notebook.
   (b) She was bored by the endless arguments.

COMBINED ―――――――――――――――――――――――――

4. (a) The setter wagged its tail happily.
   (b) It was delighted at its master's return.

COMBINED: ―――――――――――――――――――――――――

5. (a) Alice planned a quick divorce.
   (b) She was shocked by the revelations in her husband's secret diary.

COMBINED: ―――――――――――――――――――――――――

6. (a) Fred tore up his paper and started all over.
   (b) Fred was unhappy with the first draft.

COMBINED: ―――――――――――――――――――――――――

Here are *three* sentences to combine. You will need a comma *and* a conjunction.

7. (a) Archimedes rushed through the streets crying "Eureka!"
   (b) Archimedes was elated with his discovery.
   (c) Archimedes was unaware that he had nothing on. (and)

COMBINED: ―――――――――――――――――――――――――

This time you have to supply the second sentence before you write the combined sentence. In set 10, you will have to write the second *and* third.

8. (a) The team celebrated its great victory.

   (b) _____

COMBINED: _____

---

9. (a) It is clearly the oldest house on the street.

   (b) _____

COMBINED: _____

---

10. (a) The general praised his troops.

   (b) _____ (and)

   (c) _____

COMBINED: _____

Note: The section titled "Improving Sentence Style" (pages 117–118) contains some cautions about dangling phrases.

CHANGING VERB FORMS

Verbs that express the *past* can be changed to the *present* by adding "-ing" to them (making them present participles) in order to combine two sentences.

> **Example**
> (a) Jerry made out his will.
> (b) Jerry thought he would not survive. (-ING)
> COMBINED: Thinking he would not survive, Jerry made out his will.

EXERCISE 11

INSTRUCTIONS: 1. The first sentence will always remain the same (except for the opening capital letter).
2. Change the verb in the second sentence to an "-ing" word, and put the second sentence in front.
3. Cross out words that repeat.
4. Insert a comma.
5. Be sure that the person (noun or pronoun) doing the action comes directly after the comma.

This one is done for you:

(a) Susan tore through the book.
(b) Susan tried to come up with the answer. (ING)

> COMBINED: *Trying to come up with the answer,* Susan tore through the book.

1. (a) She walked serenely toward the stage and accepted the award.
   (b) She ignored all their hostile looks. (ING)

COMBINED: _____

2. (a) The old trapper looked up and saw smoke curling from his cabin's chimney.
   (b) The trapper stumbled along as best he could. (ING)

COMBINED: _____

3. (a) The Cardinals decided that they had no chance to win.
   (b) The Cardinals lost track of the score.

COMBINED: _____

4. (a) Sol discovered that his tools were safe.
   (b) Sol lit a match to illuminate the cellar.

COMBINED: _____

5. (a) Mike stepped out of the sauna.
   (b) Mike glowed with health and charm.

COMBINED: _____

6. (a) The church dominates the town's center.
   (b) The church stands tall above the other buildings.

COMBINED: _____

Now make up the second sentence yourself and then combine it with the first.

7. (a) He rushed through the crowded luggage department.

   (b) _____

COMBINED: _____

8. (a) The lookout cried "Land! Land!"

    (b) _____

    _____

COMBINED: _____

_____

Now make up all three parts on your own.

9. (a) _____

    _____

    (b) _____

    _____

COMBINED: _____

_____

10. (a) _____

    _____

    (b) _____

    _____

COMBINED: _____

_____

Note: Turn to Exercise 21 in Chapter 4 for more work with dangling phrases.

ADDING DESCRIPTIVE "WHO" AND "WHOSE" WORD GROUPS

Everyone can add descriptive words to a sentence. This unit will show you how to add whole groups of words that describe people, things, or ideas in combined sentences.

Example

    The man greeted us warmly.

Can you add a descriptive word to "man"? How about "old"?

    The <u>old</u> man greeted us warmly.

But suppose you wanted to say that <u>the man wore a red jacket</u>? Then the series would look like this:

(a) The man greeted us warmly.

(b) The man wore a red jacket. (who)

COMBINED: The man <u>who wore a red jacket</u> greeted us warmly.

Here is another example:
(a) The woman owned the house.
(b) The woman wore a green coat. (who)
COMBINED: The woman <u>who wore a green coat</u> owned the house.
Notice that no commas are necessary.

EXERCISE 12

Combine these sentences:

1. (a) The man lives over there.
    (b) The man won a million dollars in the lottery last July. (WHO)

COMBINED: _____

2. (a) The general now runs a base in Alaska.
    (b) The general just got demoted. (WHO)

COMBINED: _____

3. (a) When I arrived I was met by three men.
    (b) The men claimed they were FBI agents. (WHO)
    (c) But the men refused to show me any identification. (WHO)

COMBINED: _____

4. (a) Somebody has grounds for complaining.
    (b) Her friends will not lend her any money. (WHOSE)

COMBINED: _____

5. (a) College can help a student.
    (b) The student is willing to work hard. (WHO)

COMBINED: _____

6. (a) The regulations clearly state that a person must be punished.
    (b) A person's taxes are in arrears. (WHOSE)

COMBINED: _____

In sets 7, 8, and 9, write the second sentence yourself and combine it with the sentence already supplied. In set 10, write the second and third sentences.

7. (a) An architect cannot expect to get ahead.

(b) _____

_____(WHO)

COMBINED: _____

_____

8. (a) She is a quiet woman.

(b) _____

_____(WHOSE)

COMBINED: _____

_____

9. (a) They all searched for the boy.

(b) _____

_____(WHO)

COMBINED: _____

_____

10. (a) Anyone needs help.

(b) _____

_____ (WHO)

(c) _____

_____ (AND WHO)

COMBINED: _____

_____

Note: Review the section "Concrete Language" (pages 13–22) for ways of making language more specific.

INSERTING "WITH"

The word "with" can be used to add a phrase to sentences.

Example

(a) It was a long road.
(b) The road had sharp turns.
COMBINED: It was a long road with sharp turns.

EXERCISE 13

Sets 1 through 5 have two or more parts to combine.
1. (a) Her dentist drives a 1958 Ferrari 250GT.

(b) It has a six-cylinder engine. (WITH)

(c) It has a body by Pinin Farina. (AND)

COMBINED: _____

---

2. (a) They ran into a huge collie.

   (b) The collie had a long coat. (WITH)

   (c) The collie had floppy ears. (,)

   (d) It had a ferocious bark. (, AND)

COMBINED: _____

---

3. (a) There it stood, a perfect example of an antique colonial house.

   (b) There was a fan window.

   (c) It had a center chimney

   (d) The ceilings were low.

COMBINED: _____

---

4. (a) I remember my favorite children's books.

   (b) They had lovable elves.

   (c) There were evil godmothers.

   (d) There were handsome princes.

   (e) They had happy endings.

COMBINED: _____

---

5. (a) Jenkins was the most decorated officer on the force.

   (b) Jenkins had three medals for bravery.

   (c) Jenkins had seven citations for good conduct.

COMBINED: _____

EXERCISE 14

Try reversing the order now. Take set 5 in Exercise 13 and see what happens when the "with" phrase comes first:

> With three medals for bravery and seven citations for good conduct, Jenkins was the most decorated officer on the force.

In many sentences there will be a choice; the "with" phrase can go before or after sentence (a). Do sets 1 and 2 both ways, the "with" before and after.

1. (a) Shelly looked like a model.
   (b) She had long, slim legs.
   (c) She had expressive eyes.
   (d) She had silky hair.

COMBINED: ("with" after) _____

_____

_____

COMBINED: ("with" before) _____

_____

2. (a) Manny looks terrible.
   (b) He has bags under his eyes.
   (c) His hair is unkept
   (d) His clothes are rumpled.

COMBINED: ("with" after) _____

_____

_____

COMBINED: ("with" before) _____

_____

Now put the "with" phrases in the middle for sets 3, 4, and 5.
3. (a) Sal's diner is getting more popular every day.
   (b) It has great steaks.
   (c) The hamburgers are cheap.
   (d) The french fries are crisp.

COMBINED: _____

4. (a) Switzerland attracts visitors who like natural beauty.
   (b) There are mighty glaciers. (WITH ITS)
   (c) Switzerland has towering mountains. (,)
   (d) The lakes are spectacular. (, AND)

COMBINED: _____

_____

_____

5. (a) The British generals in World War I thought tanks and machine guns were just passing fads; they preferred to rely on cavalry.
   (b) Their lack of foresight was typical.

COMBINED: _____

_____

_____

Note: Turn to page 14 for hints on making language more specific.

USING "WHO" AND "WHICH" PHRASES

You can add phrases beginning with "who" or "which" to combine sentences. As you proceed, you will find that you can also add phrases simply by setting them off with commas.

Example

(a) The king's tomb only succeeded in making people laugh.
(b) It was meant to impress the public. (WHICH)
COMBINED: The king's tomb, which was meant to impress the public, only succeeded in making people laugh.

Since the phrases you will add contain extra or nonessential information, surround them by commas.

EXERCISE 15

1. (a) *The Rex* had a brief but glorious career.
   (b) *The Rex* was an ocean liner designed to sail the Atlantic in five days. (WHICH)

COMBINED: _____

_____

2. (a) My friend Parker stopped by yesterday.
   (b) Parker is a sculptor. (WHO)

COMBINED: _____

_____

3. (a) Early slave narratives contain a rich store of information on Afro-American history.
   (b) They are still relatively unknown. (WHICH)

COMBINED: _____

_____

Now try combining the sentences in the following sets exactly as you did in set 2 above, except leave out the WHO or WHICH. Here is how set 2 would look:

My friend Parker, a sculptor, stopped by yesterday.

4.　(a) Buster Keaton died penniless and alone, forgotten by Hollywood.
　　(b) He was perhaps the greatest comedian of the century.

COMBINED: _____

5.　(a) *Paradise Lost* was written by a blind poet who dictated it to his daughters.
　　(b) It is the most famous epic in English.

COMBINED: _____

6.　(a) Lead is less valuable than titanium.
　　(b) Lead is one of the heaviest metals.
　　(c) Titanium is one of the lightest metals.

COMBINED: _____

7.　(a) The B-17 bomber was the mainstay of the United States Army Air Force at the beginning of World War II.
　　(b) It was nicknamed "The Flying Fortress."

COMBINED: _____

8.　(a) Paris still dictates what many men and women wear.
　　(b) Paris is the fashion capitol of the world.

COMBINED: _____

9.　(a) Jazz and the Blues both grew out of the experience of American blacks.
　　(b) Jazz and the Blues are two of the best art forms created in this country.

COMBINED: _____

10.　(a) My neighborhood borders some of the richest farmland in the state.
　　(b) My neighborhood is a solidly middle-class collection of garden apartments and ranch houses.

COMBINED: _____

SUBSTITUTING WITH "WH" WORDS

Sentences can be combined by adding the "WH" words (WHO, WHAT, WHEN, WHERE, WHETHER, WHY, HOW).

Example
(a) The scientists could not figure out *something*.
(b) The strange radio signals came from *somewhere*. (WHERE)
COMBINED: The scientists could not figure out where the strange radio signals came from.

EXERCISE 16

1. (a) No politician seems to know *something*.
   (b) One million dollars was spent on furnishing the mayor's office. (WHY)

COMBINED: _____

_____

2. (a) A smart coach knows *something*.
   (b) The players need a time out. (WHEN)

COMBINED: _____

_____

3. (a) Salmon may travel thousands of miles, but they never forget *something*.
   (b) They were born *somewhere*. (WHERE)

COMBINED: _____

_____

4. (a) By now everyone should have learned *something*.
   (b) Irreparable damage results when hasty decisions are made about the environment. (WHAT)

COMBINED: _____

_____

5. (a) Watching her sleep, they were not sure of *something*.
   (b) She would wake up recovered from the high fever. (WHETHER)

COMBINED: _____

_____

6. (a) After pounding the gavel for five minutes, the chairman asked *something*.
   (b) The delegates would come to order *sometime*. (WHEN)

COMBINED: _____

_____

7. (a) Anne never told her teacher *something*.
    (b) She missed so many classes. (WHY)

COMBINED: _____

_____

8. (a) Moving men always need directions about *something*.
    (b) They should place furniture *somewhere*. (WHERE)

COMBINED: _____

_____

9. (a) It took the committee months to decide *something*.
    (b) They should start building the office. (WHEN TO)

COMBINED: _____

_____

10. (a) Since she was new in town, she did not know *something*.
    (b) She could have the electricity turned on. (HOW)

COMBINED: _____

_____

INSERTING "THAT" AS A CONNECTOR

You can combine two sentences by replacing *something* with a "that" and adding sentence (b).

Example

(a) The pilots all knew *something*.
(b) Hopkins had been drinking. (THAT)
COMBINED: The pilots all knew that Hopkins had been drinking.

EXERCISE 17

In 1 through 5, sentence (b) follows (a).
1. (a) It did not take Perry long to discover *something*.
    (b) His car was a lemon. (THAT)

COMBINED: _____

_____

2. (a) Some people learn *something*.
    (b) It is never too late to change careers. (THAT)

COMBINED: _____

_____

3. (a) We were all astounded to find *something*.
   (b) Prices had doubled since our last trip to Italy. (THAT)

COMBINED: _____

_____

4. (a) The office manager immediately understood *something*.
   (b) Perkins could not be trusted to keep the lunch orders straight. (THAT)

COMBINED: _____

_____

5. (a) The police officer testified *something*.
   (b) She saw the car hit the tree. (THAT)

COMBINED: _____

_____

Now replace *something* with THE FACT THAT and put (b) before (a).
6. (a) *Something* intrigued the detective.
   (b) There were no footprints. (THE FACT THAT)

COMBINED: _____

_____

7. (a) *Something* was apparent to the commuters.
   (b) The train would never arrive. (THE FACT THAT)

COMBINED: _____

_____

8. (a) *Something* meant little to her.
   (b) He tried his best. (THE FACT THAT)

COMBINED: _____

_____

In the next sets, add the second sentence yourself before you do the combining.
9. (a) The Romans all believed *something*.

   (b) _____ (THAT)

COMBINED: _____

_____

10. (a) Everyone said *something*.

    (b) _____ (THAT)

COMBINED: _____

_____

SUBSTITUTING "IT" AND ADDING "THAT"

Sentences can be combined by putting an "it" in place of *something* in the first sentence and a "that" before the second sentence. Sometimes you will need to change the order or omit words.

Example
(a) *Something* is obvious.
(b) We cannot go on meeting like this. (IT . . . THAT)
COMBINED: It is obvious that we cannot go on meeting like this.

EXERCISE 18

1. (a) *Something* bothered me.
   (b) I never had any friends my own age. (IT . . . THAT)

COMBINED: _____

_____

2. (a) *Something* occurred to Peter.
   (b) Melody might not be answering the phone because she was out with another man.

COMBINED: _____

_____

3. (a) Although she was an experienced banker, *something* surprised her.
   (b) Her promotion came so rapidly.

COMBINED: _____

_____

4. (a) *Something* amused him when he thought about it.
   (b) He thought no one knew his secret.

COMBINED: _____

_____

5. (a) To learn *something* was no great shock.
   (b) The bottle of pills was half-empty.

COMBINED: _____

_____

6. (a) Since the store was such a crowded place, *something* was surprising to discover.
   (b) It had been losing money for years.

COMBINED: _____

_____

7. (a) *Something* told the psychologist *something*.
   (b) I dreamed of a long train trip. (THE FACT THAT)
   (c) I want to escape my present situation. (THAT)

COMBINED: _____

In sets 8, 9, and 10, start the combination with the word "that." (Cross out extra words.)

8. (a) There is a life after death.
   (b) That is something most religious people believe.

COMBINED: *That* _____

---

9. (a) He arrived home after six o'clock.
   (b) It is clearly established by the evidence.

COMBINED: *That* _____

---

10. (a) Margie will get promoted.
    (b) It is unlikely.

COMBINED: *That* _____

CHAPTER 6

WORD ENDINGS

The Apostrophe "s" Ending

The usual way of indicating that someone owns something is to put an apostrophe (') and an "s" after the owner's name: Geraldine's house; Anna's snowmobile. The apostrophe "s" shows that the house belongs to Geraldine and the snowmobile belongs to Anna.

The same ending applies to objects and ideas as well as people: the cat's meow; yesterday's paper; today's world; the dawn's early light.

EXERCISE 1

Place an apostrophe and an "s" in the following sentences. (Some of them already have the "s" but not the apostrophe.)
  1. Allans sailboat is in Frank cellar this winter.
  2. After they had accepted the ride, they noticed that Sallys luggage had been left behind at the bus stop.
  3. One of their house best features was the row of 65-foot elms along the north side.
  4. They would have drowned except for the lifeguards quick thinking.
  5. Among Marys favorite records was a performance by Duke Ellington orchestra.
  6. Three of their cats once climbed into the trees highest branch.
  7. The shrimp salad is one of this restaurants most popular entrees.
  8. Allowances for children are steadily rising because parents see how much kids toys and candy now cost.

9. She claims that womens fashions change too often.
10. Three of the plane seats were broken.

There are three kinds of problems with the apostrophe:

1. Leaving out the apostrophe
2. Putting in extra apostrophes
3. Confusing ownership with contractions

Let's look at each one separately.

LEAVING OUT THE APOSTROPHE

For some writers the sound is what determines if a sentence is correct. This is a sensible approach, but here it cannot help because the apostrophe is never pronounced. If the "s" is present, it sounds right even though the apostrophe is missing. In writing, the apostrophe *must* be put in, and the only way to be certain is to check for ownership.

EXERCISE 2

All these sentences need one apostrophe; the "s" is already there.
1. Why does that stores awning always drip when it rains?
2. He tried as hard as he could to fix the cars tire, but the bolts were too tight and he broke his fingernails on the hubcaps.
3. She plays so rough that the other teams manager wants her suspended from the rest of the tournament.
4. His eyes blinked when he heard what his friends father had paid for the new lawn mowers.
5. The dogs bones were buried under the flowers.
6. Do you know what time the films last showing is?
7. All the young boys were gathered by the waters edge.
8. Neither Geoffrey nor Arthur wants to miss a single days pay this summer.
9. The magicians hat produced rabbits, eggs, and coins.
10. All the lottery tickets he ever bought won him only ten dollars worth of prizes.

PUTTING IN TOO MANY APOSTOPHES

People who are not very sure of apostrophes put them in whenever they are in doubt. Save them for indicating ownership.

EXERCISE 3

Remove the extra, unnecessary apostrophes in the following sentences, being careful not to remove apostrophes that belong there.

1. He alway's liked the way his aunt's airplane flew.
2. Dr. Jone's regret's that she will not be able to attend tonight's dinner party at the Spanish ambassador's.
3. That car's muffler need's replacing before the owner get's a ticket from one of the meter maid's.
4. The tree's swayed as the breeze's increased their force.
5. June's typewriter is on sale for forty dollar's.
6. When do Stan's brother's leave for the mountain's?
7. Are there any apple's left for John's dessert?
8. The radio predicted rain shower's on this morning's forecast, but I never trust what the weather report's say.
9. On his night's off, Ollie watches his favorite television show's to his heart's content.
10. The majority of this state's inhabitant's are against building any new highway's.

Checking for Ownership

One good way to find ownership is to look for the thing owned to appear right after the owner. Most of the time the word that should get the apostrophe "s" is directly followed by what is owned: Larry's sock; the team's best player.

In some cases the thing that is owned will be understood: Is this today's mail? No, it is yesterday's. Whose book is this? It is Leon's.

CONFUSING OWNERSHIP WITH CONTRACTIONS

Look at this sentence:

This street's a mess.

Is the apostrophe "s" showing ownership? No. This is a contraction, a shortening, taking place. The verb in the sentence is "is," and the letter "i" has been replaced by an apostrophe to show that it is missing. Another way of writing the sentence would be:

This street is a mess.

To say

This street's a mess

is to employ a natural form of word-shortening, called a contraction. Everyone uses contractions in speech, as in

He's my brother. or It's cold outside.

for

He is my brother. or It is cold outside.

(In most formal writing this "s" contraction should be avoided; write "He is leaving" instead of "He's leaving.") In such sentences, the apostrophe has nothing to do with ownership; it simply indicates that a letter has been left out. That is the source of confusion over <u>it's</u> (it is) and <u>its</u>; <u>let's</u> (let us) and <u>lets</u>; and <u>there's</u> (there is) and <u>theirs</u>.

EXERCISE 4

Add the missing apostrophes.
1. There are all sorts of birds in these trees, but the buildings blocking my view of them.
2. Hes sailing in two days, and he'll be gone as long as theres money in his pockets.
3. Theres no business like show business.
4. Lets see if he lets us use his brother skis.
5. The chemistry lessons over in ten minutes, so she'll be leaving from one of that buildings main exits.
6. There doesnt seem to be any real purpose to running three miles every afternoon.
7. The reason shes poor is that shes too honest to work at jobs she doesnt believe in.
8. He said, "Lets see what happens if you take those two chemicals and mix them together."
9. If shes in town tonight, why dont you give her a call?
10. Since its too late for a movie, lets just take a walk in the park.

POSSESSIVE PRONOUNS

Take this example of a possessive pronoun:

Susan brought <u>her</u> own coat.

The only other way to write this sentence would be:

Susan brought Susan's own coat.

Notice that to replace the "her" you would have to use "Susan's" with an apostrophe. The word "her" does not get an apostrophe "s" because it is *already* possessive; it is a possessive pronoun.

Other possessive pronouns are familiar to you: my, your, his, its, our, their. Sometimes some of these words get an "s" added to them for the purpose of making a sentence sound smoother. Even so, they *never* take an apostrophe.

Example
That is your book/That book is yours. Is this one of hers? It's theirs. Can I try some of yours?

Possessive Pronouns

	SINGULAR		PLURAL
Pronoun	*Possessive*	*Pronoun*	*Possessive*
I	my, mine	we	our, ours
you	your, yours	you	your, yours
he	his		
she	her, hers	they	their, theirs
it	its		

The following pronouns are not possessive; they take an apostrophe "s" just like other words:

one/one's   somebody/somebody's   nobody/nobody's
someone/someone's   anybody/anybody's   everyone/everyone's
anyone/anyone's   everybody/everybody's

Example

It's anybody's guess. Is this someone's idea of a joke? It's best not to count one's chickens before they're hatched.

EXERCISE 5

Add the missing apostrophes.
1. That is nobodys business but yours.
2. Someones cat caught its tail in my rose bushes.
3. That friend of yours looks in everyones window.
4. If anybodys house gets robbed, you can be sure it won't be theirs.
5. If it isn't hers, its someone elses.
6. That ten dollar bill isn't ours, but it must be someones.
7. If anyones arm got twisted, I'm sure it wasn't yours.
8. In those days, everybodys troubles soon became ours.
9. One had better watch ones language in this part of town.
10. My sisters would not waste their precious time at just anybodys party.

The "-s" Ending on Verbs

The letter "s" on a verb indicates that the subject is singular. The rule is:

Rule

If the subject is third person singular, that is, a noun, pronoun, word, or phrase that can be replaced by "he," "she," or "it," . . .
Add "s" to the verb if the action is going on now or goes on as a habit (that is, verbs in the present).

Put another way, an "s" on a verb *always* shows that the subject is singular.

Examples

I <u>walk</u> home every day. (Rule does not apply—not "he," "she," or "it.")
Harry <u>walks</u> home every day. (Rule applies—"he.")
Harry <u>walked</u> home every day. (Rule does not apply—past, not present.)

The rule only applies when both conditions are there:
1. "he," "she," "it," or a word that replaces them (like "Harry")
2. present time (not the past or the future)

Examples

Rule applies:	The mailman <u>walks</u> home every day.
	He <u>walks</u> home every day.
Rule does not apply:	The mailmen <u>walk</u> home every day.
	They <u>walk</u> home every day.

The wom<u>an</u> <u>lives</u> in an old shanty. (singular; so +"s")
The wom<u>en</u> <u>live</u> in an old shanty. (plural; so no "s")
The <u>car</u> <u>uses</u> unleaded fuel. (singular; so +"s")
The <u>cars</u> <u>use</u> unleaded fuel. (plural; so no "s")

EXERCISE 6

Choose the right form of the verb.
1. This stove get/gets too hot.
2. My brother's friend drink/drinks rum.
3. They all ride/rides ten-speed bicycles.
4. Sheila never like/likes to hitchhike.
5. This book cost/costs too much, so I won't buy it.
6. When a worm appear/appears, the bird will catch it.
7. That dress suit/suits her well.
8. All that dust get/gets in my eyes.
9. Too many people look/looks tired.
10. Those cats just sit/sits and wait/waits.

APPLYING THE "S" RULE

1. The rule only applies to verbs referring to present time. The ending for the past is, of course, "-ed."
2. Some verbs change their spelling to follow the rule:

I am	I have	I do	I try
you are	you have	you do	you try
he is	he has	he does	he tries
she is	she has	she does	she tries
it is	it has	it does	it tries

3. Some verbs *never* add the "s": can, could, may, might, must, ought, shall, will, would. These are the only ones.
4. When there is a compound verb—a main verb plus helping verbs (auxiliaries)—the main verb never gets the "s." Instead, change the helping verbs.

I have been here for hours.   Are you going home?
He has been here for hours.   Is she going home?

5. When a sentence begins with "there," the subject comes *after* the verb; check for the subject before writing the verb:

There are two errors.   There is my coat.
There is one error.   There are my coats.

Note: Only one past verb ever changes: was/were. He was late; you were late; they were late; we were late.

EXERCISE 7

Fill in the right form of verb in the spaces provided. Remember to keep all verbs in the present; don't add "ed."

1. Albert said, "Larry ＿＿＿ to buy a stereo." (WANT)

2. ＿＿＿ he tried looking up their address? (HAVE)

3. When my father ＿＿＿ a vacation, he ＿＿＿ all day long. (TAKE, FISH)

4. If she doesn't know the answer, she usually ＿＿＿ it up in the dictionary. (LOOK)

5. That jacket ＿＿＿ to fit you well. (SEEM)

6. When ＿＿＿ this train get to Chicago? (DO)

7. How long ＿＿＿ he been waiting here? (HAVE)

8. Tell her that she ＿＿＿ too much hot water. (USE)

9. Because he never ＿＿＿ Houston, I never ＿＿＿ a chance to see him. (VISIT, GET)

10. Make sure that picture _____ up properly with all the others on the wall. (LINE)

EXERCISE 8

Contractions (words with a letter replaced by an apostrophe) also follow the rule. Underline the right word.
1. He don't/doesn't take anybody's advice.
2. There's/there are the woman who say/says she want/wants to be president.
3. This knife don't/doesn't cut cleanly.
4. Haven't/hasn't it been three years since we met?
5. There are/is some people who haven't/hasn't filled out the forms properly.
6. There's/there are two kinds of pictures I admire.
7. When's/when are the bars closing?
8. One of my friends don't/doesn't know how to drive.
9. They wasn't/weren't worth the money.
10. Buy me a paper while you are out, unless they are/is all gone.

If you had trouble with any of those exercises, remember which ones and concentrate on them. They are all common examples of the "s" rule; they will continue to give you problems unless you master them right away.

One cause for trouble might be that the "s" is not always pronounced. Listen to yourself read the correct answers to Exercise 6, or ask someone to listen to you. If your speech pattern tends to leave out the final "s" in words, you will have to be especially careful in writing. You won't be able to tell if the "s" is missing or present by reading your paper aloud.

WORDS BETWEEN SUBJECT AND VERB

One major problem with the "s" ending comes from words that appear between the subject and the verb. Look at these sentences:

1. One of her best friends work there.
2. The cause of these storms are tropical disturbances down in the Caribbean.
3. The box of chocolates sit on the table.

These sentences are all wrong! In each case the subject requires an "s" on the end of the verb. Look at them again: in number 1, who does the work? "One of her best friends," not all of them. The subject is singular, so the verb must have an "s":

1(a). One of her best friends works there.

In number 2 the subject is "cause," so the verb must be the singular, "is":

> 2(a). The <u>cause</u> of these storms <u>is</u> tropical disturbances in the Caribbean.

Can you find the subject in number 3? Write it in:

_____.

How should the sentence be rewritten?

> 3(a). _____.

Do not let words that come between the subject and verb fool you; the subject itself, wherever it is in the sentence, will determine whether or not the verb in the present gets an "s."

Some words look plural, seem to refer to more than one person, but are nevertheless singular:

everybody	everyone	each
somebody	someone	either
nobody	no one	neither
anybody	anyone	

All those words force the present verb to add an "s."

Examples

<u>Is</u> everybody happy? <u>Does</u> anyone care? Nobody <u>is</u> home. Either one <u>is</u> fine with me. Each <u>is</u> different.

(Notice that you can't write "Are everybody happy?" or "Each are different." The words require the "s.")

EXERCISE 9

Rewrite the following sentences, making all the necessary corrections, but do *not* add words or change verbs to the past.

1. If either of the fighters get hurt, the referee will declare a technical knockout.

   _____

   _____

2. The most important women in my family is the ones who has a career.

   _____

   _____

3. Mick and Linda harvests their corn by hand.

   _____

   _____

4. When the train pull out of the station, make sure she see you wave.

_____

_____

5. My sister always ask what something cost before she buy it.

_____

_____

6. Everybody, especially my brothers, like coffee after dinner.

_____

_____

7. The inspector with the blue sunglasses always look carefully at travelers who comes from Cuba.

_____

_____

8. Make sure that everybody who want a second helping have a chance to get one.

_____

_____

9. One of my brothers don't like to swim when the water is below fifty degrees.

_____

_____

10. Neither my sister nor her roommate ever go to a singles bar.

_____

_____

EXERCISE 10

Rewrite the following sentences. Change the underlined word from the plural to the singular, and make all the other necessary alterations. Do not change the verbs to the past. The first one is done for you:

1. Snowstorms make familiar places look strange and different.

   A snowstorm makes familiar places look strange and different.

2. He told me that two of his friends use dandruff shampoo.

_____

_____

3. The <u>people</u> who live down the road never go out after dark.

   _____

   _____

4. <u>Flowers</u> bought from a florist never make the same impression as <u>flowers</u> you pick yourself.

   _____

   _____

5. Geology <u>books</u> that have fancy illustrations usually cost over ten dollars.

   _____

   _____

6. The <u>women</u> next door always walk their dogs after dinner.

   _____

   _____

7. <u>Cars</u> that use huge quantities of gasoline will not sell very well in the future.

   _____

   _____

8. <u>Swimming pools</u> serve as status symbols in many parts of the world.

   _____

   _____

9. Detergent <u>commercials</u> are the worst annoyances of television.

   _____

   _____

10. <u>Newspapers</u> with good international coverage are getting harder to find.

   _____

   _____

Summary

The sign of the <u>plural in nouns</u> is usually "s" (book, book<u>s</u>; car, car<u>s</u>).
In <u>verbs</u>, the only time an "s" gets added is <u>in the singular</u> if two conditions are met:
1. The verb is in the present (no "ed" or "will").
2. The subject is "he," "she," "it," or a word that can replace them (third person).

The "-ed" Ending on Verbs

There are three main occasions when the addition of an "-ed" ending is important:

1. On verbs—to show that an action took place in the past.
2. In compound verbs—when the main verb is preceded by "be," "become," "get," or "have."
3. On descriptive words (adjectives) formed from verbs.

Let's look at each specific use of the "-ed" ending.

ACTION IN THE PAST

A good definition of a verb is that it is a word that changes to show time. Take the verb "look":

> 1. They <u>look</u> at every passing girl.

This is the *present*; it shows what they *are doing* now, or what they usually *do*, which is "look."

> 2. They <u>looked</u> at every passing girl.

This is the *past*; it shows what they *did*, which was "looked." The only way to tell when the looking occurred is by noting the "-ed" on "looked." Otherwise, you wouldn't know. Here is another example:

> 4. I <u>want</u> to eat that layer cake.
> 5. I <u>wanted</u> to eat that layer cake.

From the endings you can tell if the cake is still around. Is the cake still there in sentence 4? How about in sentence 5? How can you tell? The answer is: from the "-ed" and only from the "-ed."

If you tend to leave the "-ed" out—and here the essays your instructor has returned to you will be your best guide—you will have to be especially careful. Reading your paper aloud might not always help, for certain speech patterns omit many "-ed" endings. Many people drop the "-ed" when the next word begins with the letter "t," as in:

> I <u>used to</u> live in St. Louis.

Here the "used to" is often pronounced "yoosta" and sometimes written "use to" by mistake. If you have written it this way, or if you leave out the "-ed" in other situations, practice the exercises that follow and check your papers carefully for signs of verbs in the past. Every regular English verb needs an "-ed" to form the past.

EXERCISE 11

A verb in the past needs to be inserted in each of the following sentences. The present form of the verb is provided at the end; change it to the past and put it in the blank space.

1. I lit the match, illuminating the darkness that _____ me on all sides. (SURROUND)

2. He _____ for this morning's mail. (ASK)

3. The train _____ into the station. (ROLL)

4. After dinner he _____ a big cigar. (SMOKE)

5. She _____ about where she was on the night of the murder. (LIE)

6. One of the bullets _____ the woodchuck. (KILL)

7. They _____ them down to the station. (MARCH)

8. We _____ at it, but we never _____ her name. (WORK, RE-MEMBER)

9. Allen, my best friend, _____ late for the wedding. (ARRIVE)

10. The old mansion _____ out over miles of dark forests. (LOOK)

EXERCISE 12

Change each of the following sentences to the past.

1. Mr. Luzinski always arrives on time.

   _____

   _____

2. They all want to go to the beach.

   _____

   _____

3. He talks on the telephone for hours.

   _____

   _____

4. At nine o'clock I usually walk the dog.

_____

_____

5. We all use too many misspelled words.

_____

_____

6. The neighbor's child always climbs our tree.

_____

_____

7. A Greek cook never uses butter; olive oil serves the same purpose and imparts its own special flavor.

_____

_____

8. Carlos laughs whenever he recalls Larry's jokes.

_____

_____

9. They all hope to see their relatives.

_____

_____

10. We fry everything in our restaurant.

_____

_____

Note: Some verbs, as you see in your answer to number 10, undergo certain spelling changes to form the past. The rules are:

> If it ends in "e," add "d."
> If it ends in "y," change the "y" to "i" and add "ed."

(Other verbs, called *irregular verbs* because they do not follow the "-ed" rule, form the past by changing one or more of their internal letters. Thus, "is" becomes "was"; "drink," "drank"; "do," "did"; "sit," "sat." With few exceptions, these verbs present little trouble. Specific problems with them are treated in the next section of this chapter; there is also a reference list of irregular verbs on pages 167–168.)

COMPOUND VERBS

Another use of the "-ed" ending concerns verbs preceded by "be," "become," "get, " or "have." Here is the rule for regular verbs (the ones that change by means of the "-ed" ending):

Rule

Any one or any
combination of
these words

SUBJECT +

be
am
is
are
was
were
being
been
become
became
becoming
get
getting
got
have
has
had
having

+ VERB + -ED ending

Here are some examples of the rule in action:

Frank + is   + injure + -ED = Frank is injured.
Rita + got   + fire   + -ED = Rita got fired.
A man + has been + kill   + -ED = A man has been killed.

If you leave off the "-ed," you have broken the rule.

The rule for irregular verbs is exactly the same as the rule for regular verbs, except that the irregular verbs change their spelling instead of adding "-ed." (A few don't change at all: cost, has cost.)

Her foot + has been + bite + spelling change = Her foot has been bitten.
The bread + has   + rise + spelling change = The bread has risen.
The car   + was   + steal + spelling change = The car was stolen.

The grammatical term for the "-ed" ending or the spelling change is *past participle*, so the rule could also be stated this way:

SUBJECT + (be, become, get, or have) + verb + past participle.

This is a list of some common irregular verbs with the spelling changes that transform them to the past and the past participle.

Present	Past	Past Participle
begin	began	begun
bend	bent	bent
bite	bit	bitten
blow	blew	blown
break	broke	broken

bring	brought	brought
build	built	built
buy	bought	bought
catch	caught	caught
choose	chose	chosen
deal	dealt	dealt
dive	dived, dove	dived
do	did	done
draw	drew	drawn
drive	drove	driven
drink	drank	drunk
eat	ate	eaten
fall	fell	fallen
fly	flew	flown
freeze	froze	frozen
give	gave	given
go	went	gone
grow	grew	grown
hide	hid	hidden
know	knew	known
lend	lent	lent
lay (put, place)	laid	laid
lie (recline)	lay	lain
lose	lost	lost
ride	rode	ridden
ring	rang	rung
rise	rose	risen
run	ran	run
shake	shook	shaken
shrink	shrank	shrunk, shrunken
sing	sang	sung
sink	sank	sunk
sit	sat	sat
speak	spoke	spoken
stand	stood	stood
steal	stole	stolen
strike	struck	struck, stricken
swim	swam	swum
take	took	taken
teach	taught	taught
tear	tore	torn
throw	threw	thrown
wear	wore	worn
write	wrote	written

Go through the list looking for words that have given you trouble before. Which seem new to you? They are precisely the ones to be wary of. Copy the difficult words onto your spelling chart.

EXERCISE 13

Write *ten* sentences; use the past participle of the verb next to the number as the main verb.

1. (choose) _____

_____

2. (draw) _____

_____

3. (drive) _____

_____

4. (fly) _____

_____

5. (know) _____

_____

6. (rise) _____

_____

7. (shrink) _____

_____

8. (sink) _____

_____

9. (throw) _____

_____

10. (write) _____

_____

EXERCISE 14

Fill in the blank with the correct form of the verb.

1. Is that seat _____? (TAKE)
2. Their driveway was _____ from view. (HIDE)
3. Indians had _____ about the Mississippi long before the Europeans arrived. (KNOW)
4. They have _____ some quinine water. (BUY)

5. They have _____ some quinine water. (BRING)

6. Has the second act _____ yet? (BEGIN)

7. Many are called, but few are _____. (CHOOSE)

8. All the clothing has been _____ away. (GIVE)

9. Two watches and four bracelets were _____. (STEAL)

10. Here is a letter that was _____ by Shakespeare. (WRITE)

DESCRIPTIVE WORDS FORMED FROM VERBS

Descriptive words (adjectives) are often formed from the past participles of verbs. They either have the familiar "-ed" ending or, if the verb is irregular, the spelling change. Here are some examples:

> a radio dispatched cab; french fried potatoes; whipped cream; newly fallen snow; shrunken head

Be especially careful not to drop off the "-ed" ending from these words. Did you know that "whipped cream" had an "-ed"? Many people leave it off by mistake.

EXERCISE 15

Fill in the right word. The verbs from which the descriptive words must be formed are at the end of the sentences.

1. That house has a poorly _____ garage. (PAINT)

2. Who wants a _____ cheese sandwich? (GRILL)

3. It may be only a _____ Buick, but Karen loves it. (USE)

4. My advice is to avoid _____ foods and _____ vegetables. (FRY; OVERCOOK)

5. The book lay on the highly _____ table. (POLISH)

6. The lookout tower, _____ up the mountain on the backs of struggling porters, now stands _____. (CARRY; DESERT)

7. Clark emerged half- _____ from the crowd, but he had the autograph. (TRAMPLE)

8. _____ to wait patiently, Yvette browsed through some _____ magazines. (TELL; DISCARD)

9. The bullet- _____ sign proclaimed in bold letters, "No Hunting." (RIDDLE)

10. The cannon was _____ , _____, and _____ in one quick motion. (LOAD; PRIME; FIRE)

EXERCISE 16

Put the correct form of "use" or "suppose" in the following sentences.

1. Aren't we _____ to be in Wyoming by now? (SUPPOSE)
2. I do not want to _____ my sauna. (USE)
3. They never _____ to sell rug shampoo. (USE)
4. I never would have _____ you'd like *Scrabble*. (SUPPOSE)
5. They wanted crisp new bills, not old _____ ones. (USE)
6. What do you _____ he meant by that? (SUPPOSE)
7. Are sleeping cars still in _____ on this railroad? (USE)
8. There _____ to be more trouble getting in. (USE)
9. I never _____ a toothpick anymore. (USE)
10. Little children are not _____ to be up so late. (SUPPOSE)

MASTERY TEST I FOR WORD ENDINGS

The following sentences have errors in the use of word endings (apostrophe "s," "s" on verbs, and "-ed" on verbs). Rewrite them, making all the appropriate corrections. Keep all present verbs in the present.

1. In winter a persons vision is affect by the snows glare.

_____

_____

2. One of my sisters friends live there.

_____

_____

3. The current economic conditions makes it difficult for the mattress factory to hire any new employees.

_____

_____

4. In trial's, all twelve jurors have to agreed on the verdict.

_____

_____

5. Drugs is a great temptation to poor young person's who dont have jobs.

_____

_____

6. Joan's parents have never accept the fact that she want to be a farmer.

_____

_____

7. Juliet was suppose to return her sons ski's this morning.

_____

_____

8. If they had move to Houston, they would not have to worry about cold winter's.

_____

_____

9. St. Francis of Assisi once deliver a sermon to a flock of bird's.

_____

_____

10. Todays clothing styles emphasizes informality.

_____

_____

MASTERY TEST II FOR WORD ENDINGS

Rewrite these sentences, making all the appropriate corrections, and keeping present verbs in the present.

1. These book's costs seven dollar's to replace.

_____

_____

2. The Treasurers Reports was not detail enough.

_____

_____

3. One companys advertisements use to claim that their cabs were all radio dispatch.

_____

_____

4. All the days mail was waiting for her, carefully open, sorted, and arrange neatly on the desk.

_____

_____

5. The gas station I use has the lowest price's I know of.

_____

_____

6. Their's was the neatest house on the block, except for our neighbors.

_____

_____

7. Her hair look wind-blowed, just like in the movies.

_____

_____

8. Hard pack snow is best for making snowball's.

_____

_____

9. The drink have a thinly slice bit of orange rind and two cherrie's.

_____

_____

10. His newspaper give him more than fifteen cents worth of entertainment.

_____

_____

CHAPTER 7

PUNCTUATION AND CAPITAL LETTERS

Commas

Five common occasions require a comma:

Rule 1

Place a comma
   A. After every item in an address: Chicago, Illinois; Rome, Italy, is my home at present.
   B. Between the date and year or the day and month: April 7, 1968; Tuesday, March 1.
   C. Between parts of measurements: seven pounds, one ounce; chapter six, verse fourteen.
   D. Before quotations introduced by verb forms of saying: He said, "I did it."

EXERCISE 1

Put commas in the following sentences:
1. Harry Truman lived in Independence Missouri.
2. She was born on April 1 1975 weighing eight pounds eleven ounces.
3. Patrick Henry said "Give me liberty or give me death" on September 7 1775 in Richmond Virginia.

4. All of her classmates came from Medicine Hat Alberta where she grew up.
5. Six feet nine inches was his height when he started for the Lakers.

Rule 2

Place commas between equal items in a series.
   A. He gave her a radio, a phonograph, and a color television.
   B. Ms. Copley said she had turned off the lights, shut the door, and hidden the key.
   C. Jody thought Frank was insincere, dishonest, and untrustworthy.

Make sure there is a series of equal parts. Each word or phrase must relate in the same way.

   Real series: It was a dangerous, silly, and foolhardy attempt.
   No series: We all saw the angry young man.
   No series: The lawyer lost her favorite old leather briefcase.

Test for a real series by putting an "and" between the words. If the "and" doesn't make them sound awkward, there is a real series. If it's impossible to put an "and" in, don't add commas.

EXERCISE 2

Put commas in the following sentences:
1. George liked baseball basketball and swimming.
2. My favorite breakfast foods are cereal English muffins bacon and eggs and orange juice.
3. Before Alice started the car she checked the tires adjusted the mirrors and fastened her safety belt.
4. Her paper was full of crisp details precise examples and forcefully presented opinions.
5. The inmates faced a steady diet of crusts of bread mugs of thin soup and brackish water.

Rule 3

Place a comma after introductory words and phrases.
   A. Furthermore, gasoline costs too much.
      (ONE INTRODUCTORY WORD)
   B. For example, she missed class twice last week.
      (TWO-WORD INTRODUCTORY PHRASE)
   C. Smiling broadly, Scott produced the lost hat.
      (TWO-WORD INTRODUCTORY PHRASE)
   D. After a pause that must have lasted at least thirty seconds, Congresswoman Ramirez resumed her speech. (LONG INTRODUCTORY PHRASE)

EXERCISE 3

Put commas in the following sentences:
1. Finding he had only a ten dollar bill Gerry had to borrow change from his brother.
2. Frankly I just don't care.
3. To tell the truth we stayed over an hour.
4. Unless our automobile companies develop a smaller and more economical car the foreign manufacturers will increase their sales.
5. Unhappy over her lack of friends she contemplated suicide.
6. Because I got home late I missed dinner.
7. As a matter of fact I have only one sweater.
8. Unfortunately Mr. Snodgrass did not believe in banks and so kept all his money under his mattress.
9. Tired of endless snow Fred moved to Venezuela.
10. Handsome clever and rich she looked serenely about her as the ambassador kissed her hand.

Rule 4

Place a comma between sentences that are joined by AND, BUT, OR, FOR, NOR, SO, and YET (conjunctions).
   A. I woke up at ten-thirty in the morning, and by the time I got downstairs the coffee was cold.
   B. I studied as hard as I could, yet I still failed the examination.
   C. You can have some meat, but you have to eat your vegetables first.

EXERCISE 4

Place commas in the following sentences:
1. Alvin used to look through his change very carefully but he never found a rare coin.
2. Helen felt that the store charged too much and she didn't like the way the salesmen treated her.
3. In the evening he walks down to the corner store or he sits at home watching television.
4. Their farm is at the end of a long dead-end road so they have very few visitors.
5. Many Americans agree that they watch too much television yet they don't have the will power to turn the sets off and do something else instead.

Note: Look at what would happen if the word "he" were missing from the first sentence. Would you need a comma? No. There would be no reason to insert a comma because the part after the "but" would no longer be able to stand on its own as a complete sentence. The same is true of the word "she" in the second sentence.

Distinguish between independent sentences joined by a conjunction (they need the comma) and dependent phrases joined to sentences by a conjunction (no comma needed). Study the following sentences and see if you can tell which should get commas:

(a) Kim tried to rescue her brother from the rapids but she found the current too swift.

(b) Kim tried to rescue her brother from the rapids but found the current too swift.

(c) You can drive the car to my place or leave it here.

(d) You can drive the car to my place or you can leave it here.

(e) Closing his book quietly and looking over the rims of his glasses were two of Harry's most prominent mannerisms.

Rule 5

Place a comma on both sides of interrupting elements.

A. Anton, who was born in Hungary, speaks excellent English. (Do you *need* to know where he was born?)

B. My essay, it seems to me, deserves a better grade.

C. Mr. Martin, my neighbor, keeps his lawn mowed.

EXERCISE 5

Place commas on both sides of the interrupting elements in the following sentences. (Only one comma will not work; you need to *surround* the extra phrase.)

1. Terrycloth bathrobes on the other hand can absorb a great deal of moisture.

2. The voters did in spite of some odd choices elect capable representatives.

3. The speaker one of the most eminent legislators in the state rambled on for two hours.

4. Academic discourse the kind of writing demanded in college requires solid examples and clear standards of proof.

5. It was late seven o'clock before the weather finally cleared.

EXERCISE 6

Write three sentences using each of the five rules. You will have a total of fifteen sentences. Check the rules carefully if you are not sure.

EXERCISE 7

Insert commas in the following sentences.

1. The suit had a long jacket flared pants and a vest.

2. Since Russo did not want to swear out a complaint the police had to let the suspect go free.

3. They claim they want to move yet they never look for a new place to live.
4. Olive was last seen in Madison Wisconsin on April 11 1974.
5. Your insurance I'm sorry to say doesn't cover collision damage.
6. Everyone including police officers will be required to register handguns.
7. The last time I saw her she was out of work but she didn't look particularly unhappy.
8. Although I have been to France at least six times in the past four years I have never seen Paris.
9. The new baby weighed eight pounds one ounce when it was born.
10. The dialogue was to put it mildly poorly written.
11. Everything I like is either illegal immoral or fattening.
12. Undecided about a career Mary signed up for Liberal Arts and discovered philosophy.
13. Peter wore a jacket and tie to the reception but there was no doubt that he still felt uncomfortable.
14. Yesterday's rainfall was seven and a half inches but it didn't set any records.
15. The garage called and said the car needed a new battery a tune up and a wheel alignment.

Suggestions for Proofreading

Most students who have trouble with commas can be classified into two categories: those who put too many in, and those who leave too many out. Find out which group you are in. If you put in too many commas, start cutting down; if you leave them out, start adding. This solution isn't foolproof, and it will never substitute for study of the rules, but it will help. Look for a pattern and then focus on the problem area.

Common Marks of Punctuation

Besides the period (.), two other punctuation marks can end a sentence: the question mark (?) and the exclamation point (!).

QUESTION MARK (?)

Use the question mark only at the end of *direct* questions.

Example
Are you going home early? (DIRECT QUESTION)

He asked, "Are you going home early?" (direct question is within the quotation marks, so the question mark goes inside)
Did he ask if you were going home early? (DIRECT QUESTION)
He asked if I was going home early. (*not* a direct question, so no question mark)

To understand the difference between a direct question and an ordinary sentence, ask a question. Then ask someone to tell you what you asked, to rephrase the question. For instance:

Student one: What time is it? (DIRECT QUESTION)
Student two: You asked, "What time is it?" (DIRECT)
Student three: You asked for the time. (*NOT* DIRECT)
Student four: You asked what time it was. (*NOT* DIRECT)

The sentences of students three and four are not questions; they are statements, for they tell rather than ask. Sentences that *ask* get question marks; sentences that *tell* get periods.

The most common problem with question marks is leaving them out when they are necessary. If you have a habit of forgetting them, check your sentences carefully for signs of direct questions.

Signs of direct questions
1. Inverted word order. (VERB FIRST, SUBJECT SECOND)
verb
↓
<u>Does</u> he <u>work</u> there now?
          ↑
      subject

           ↓
<u>Are</u>   they <u>staying</u> here?
 ↑
verb

2. An interrogative word at the beginning. ("WH-" WORDS)

Who	Where
What	Why
When	How

These words frequently (not always) begin questions.

EXERCISE 8

Punctuate the following sentences:
1. Where do you want to go
2. Can you spare some change
3. You can spare some change, can't you
4. How he got there is no concern of mine
5. She often asked herself why she married Tom

EXCLAMATION POINT (!)

Use the exclamation point to emphasize the extraordinary nature of what has been said.

Example

Stop or I'll shoot!
They all yelled, "Fire, fire!"

The exclamation point is often overused. Save it for occasions that require it. If you find yourself using an exclamation point in every paragraph, cut down on them. Too much emphasis weakens the value of the exclamation point.

Some sentences, depending on how you want them to sound, could take a period, a question mark, or an exclamation point. Here is an example:

He ate thirty turnips.
He ate thirty turnips?
He ate thirty turnips!

Notice how the sound *and* meaning change with each different punctuation mark.

EXERCISE 9

In the following sentences, put in a period, a question mark, and an exclamation point. What changes do the different punctuation marks make in sound? In meaning?
1. The dog ate the whole pie
2. The old man died
3. You're going to eat this
4. He gave us twenty-four hours to get out of town
5. She paid sixty-five dollars for that dress

SEMICOLON (;)

Use the semicolon to link closely related statements that could also stand as complete sentences.

Example

Rainy days make George unhappy; he likes plenty of sunshine.
The army marched twenty miles; every step brought the soldiers closer to safety.
(In each of these sentences a period could replace the semicolon; in that case, the "he" and the "every" would get capital letters.)

There are two points to remember when using a semicolon:

1. The semicolon goes only between statements that could stand as complete sentences.

Avoid this usage:

He ran faster than the rest of the team; having trained on the course for ten weeks.

The statement after the semicolon could not stand on its own as a complete sentence; use a comma instead.

2. Use semicolons sparingly.

Some students who are introduced to semicolons immediately begin to sprinkle them all over their papers. Avoid overusing them.

COLON (:)

Use the colon to introduce a series or a list. It often means "such as" or "for example."

Example

He asked for the following: an axe, ten yards of rope, three tent pegs, and a canteen.
They broke up into groups: ten went with Mary, four with Calvin, and six with Felipe.

Do not use the colon in a sentence after words like "for example," "for instance," or "such as." There is no need for a colon after parts of the verb "to be" ("is," "was," "were").

EXERCISE 10

Insert the right punctuation in these sentences. (One is correct, one needs a colon, and three need semicolons.)

1. Albert took his boots off slowly and then went directly to bed.
2. The outcome was predictable no runs, no hits, no errors.
3. The corner store does well because it is open until midnight it offers unlimited credit too.
4. Set the vase on the table be sure to handle it gently.
5. Peach pie is my favorite dessert next comes cherry vanilla ice cream.

QUOTATION MARKS (" ")

Use quotation marks

1. To set off the *exact words* you are repeating.
2. To set off titles of stories, articles, poems, and other short pieces of writing.
3. To give a special sense to a word.

Exact Words You Are Repeating

In giving someone else's words, *surround* them with quotation marks.

Example

1. He said, "I hope you'll accept this ring." (EXACT WORDS)
2. He said he hoped I would accept his ring. (NOT the exact words, so no quotation marks)
3. The famous advice is "Buy low, sell high."
4. The doctor said, "Take two aspirins and call me in the morning." (Put periods and commas *inside* the quotation marks.)

To Decide What Is a Quotation

Think of a speech balloon in the funnies. Everything in the balloon, including the punctuation, is part of the quotation and so goes *inside* the quotation marks.

The king stood in his tower and announced, —————————————

————————————————————————————

From *"The Wizard of Id."* A comic strip by Johnny Hart. Copyright July 4, 1976. Distributed by Field Newspaper Syndicate.

To Set Off Titles

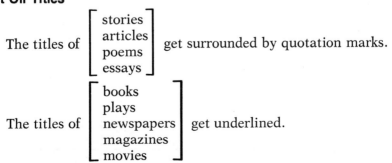

The titles of ⎡ stories / articles / poems / essays ⎤ get surrounded by quotation marks.

The titles of ⎡ books / plays / newspapers / magazines / movies ⎤ get underlined.

Example

1. I read an article in *The Los Angeles Times* called "Acupuncture and Veterinary Medicine."
2. Do you know Robert Frost's poem "Stopping by Woods on a Snowy Evening"?

(Never put quotation marks around your own title *at the top* of your essay, but do use quotation marks when you refer to your title *in the body* of the essay.)

To Give a Special Sense to a Word

Example

1. The word "ain't" appears in most dictionaries.
2. That wasn't Senator Smith's girl friend; she is his "legislative assistant."

Do not overwork this use of quotation marks. Never use them to set off a perfectly ordinary word (like "for sale") or in order to set off a slang word. Either think of another word or let it stand without quotation marks:

WRONG: We all got "busted."
RIGHT: We all got busted. We all got arrested.

Punctuating a Quotation

I said, "We don't want to buy any encyclopedias."

comma before ⟶ first letter of a quoted sentence is capitalized ⟶ end punctuation is inside

He asked, "Where is the nearest savings bank?"

Who said, "The love of money is the root of all evil"?

The entire sentence is a question, so the question mark goes *outside*.

EXERCISE 11

Write six sentences using quotation marks.
Quotation marks around exact words:

1. _____

_____

2. _____

_____

Quotation marks around a title:

3. _____

_____

4. _____

_____

Quotation marks around a word used with a special sense:

5. _____

_____

6. _____

_____

EXERCISE 12

Supply the correct punctuation for the following sentences.
1. Arlene exclaimed he's the one who stole my Labrador retriever
2. Except for three who said that they wanted to stay home, everyone agreed to take the trip to Washington
3. The salesman murmured this jacket is too loose
4. Yesterday's Daily News had a headline reading Democrats Choose New Governor
5. The coach could only manage a sad smile and a soft you win some and you lose some
6. He had never heard the word apparent used that way
7. The local people call it Heartbreak Hotel
8. Drive more carefully, dear, were the last words she said
9. He titled his first poem Outside My Window
10. One of his roommates always whistled My Bonny Lies over the Ocean during exam week

Capital Letters

Use capital letters for the following cases:

1. The first word of every sentence and quotation
2. The word "I"
3. Names of geographical and political features (everything on a map: Rocky Mountains; Red Sea; *but* a mountain; the ocean)

4. Names of streets, buildings, cities, states (everything on an envelope address: Elm Street; the Empire State Building; *but* the street after this one; that tall building)
5. Names of people and titles used in front of the name (everything on an envelope address: President Anna Gallo; Dean Green; *but* Anna Gallo, the company president; Mr. Green, the dean)
6. Names of the days, months, and holidays (everything on a calendar)
7. Names of historical eras and documents (the French Revolution; the Declaration of Independence)
8. Names of courses but *not* general subject areas (Biology 114; Nursing 301; *but* my biology class; her nursing teacher)
9. Titles of books, plays, movies, poems, articles, television shows
10. References to the Deity and names of religions
11. Brand names (a Zippo; Kellogg's Sugar Frosted Flakes)

Two kinds of writers get into difficulties over capitals: those who put extra ones in, and those who leave essential ones out. Which are you?

Those who put in extra capitals often ignore the following rule:

> *Do not use capitals for* common names of plants, animals, foods, diseases, or occupations. Example: geranium, rabbit, goldfish, spinach, lawyer, professor (unless used in a title), hay fever.

EXERCISE 13

The following sentences need at least one more capital letter. Cross out the small letter and write in a capital above it.
1. When jerome lived on eleventh street, he used to work in an italian restaurant.
2. The highest wind velocity ever recorded—over two hundred miles per hour—was on mount washington, in the white mountains of new hampshire.
3. Are you taking professor kolski's engineering class next fall?
4. The new president of the general banana company will be a. b. sampson, a retired canadian admiral.
5. She developed appendicitis during her summer at the evangelical youth alliance's camp at perry lake.
6. When I went to high school, I was required to take four years of english and history, three years of math and french, and two years of general science.
7. My place is two miles west of the entrance to smoky mountain national park.
8. Deliver the package to the armstrong building on east forty-second street between fifth and madison avenues.
9. The robins go north at the end of february.
10. She went to art school in Chicago.

MASTERY TEST I FOR PUNCTUATION AND CAPITALS

Supply the correct punctuation and capitals for the following sentences:
1. After a lengthy search madeline was hired by the chicago tribune
2. Darwin's theory of evolution first published in 1859 had an immediate impact on politics economics and religion as well as biology
3. Did you eat all the chocolate chip cookies
4. Who said war is hell
5. I can't believe i ate the whole thing
6. William James whose fame rests on his writings on philosophy education and psychology was trained as a physician.
7. Whenever the horse felt thirsty it would wander over to the pond drink some of the muddy water and gallop away
8. All her patients were poor so dr. Howell never became as wealthy as most dentists
9. Red white and blue are the colors of the american french and dutch flags
10. What are the consequences of a thyroid operation
11. As soon as it reached the crest of the hill my car sputtered shook and finally came to a stop
12. It was a double decker bus the kind they still use in england
13. The book was due at the library on august ninth a monday
14. She asked have you seen those little green pills i bought at sherman's drug store last sunday
15. They sailed for the canary islands on the third of may

MASTERY TEST II FOR PUNCTUATION AND CAPITALS

Supply the correct punctuation and capitals for the following sentences:
1. Tomorrow september 7 is my birthday
2. Your examination booklet unfortunately has disappeared
3. I said please pass the chutney
4. No one ever knew where uncle Al bought his cigars nor did they ever guess why they had such a disgusting aroma
5. A person who has a good head for figures is ambitious and can deal with customers can get this job
6. Both solutions may work but first try the more obvious one
7. Isn't one hundred dollars too much to pay for a pair of shoes
8. The ship that is docked by the jetty has never been caught in a real storm
9. underhanded sneaky and careless were three of the words he used to describe his lawyer
10. maples oaks and elms lose their leaves in the fall so they cannot possibly be thought of as evergreens
11. For harry nothing will ever replace i love lucy

12. Today's daily news has scores of all the golf matches
13. Her birthday is the same as lincolns february twelfth
14. The suspect was last seen entering the globe theater with a bodyguard
15. That is a strawberry plant the kind we used to grow back in west virginia

CHAPTER 8

THE RIGHT WORD

Contractions

A *contraction* is a word with a letter or two left out and replaced by an apostrophe (').

Think of the obvious difference between "well" and "we'll."

well	means	good, healthy
we'll	means	we will or we shall

That little apostrophe has changed the meaning and the pronunciation of the words. In fact, the apostrophe is the only way to tell them apart in writing.

CONTRACTIONS IN SPEECH

Everyone's *spoken* language makes use of contractions. These ten are some of the most familiar:

I'd	I would
you'd	you would
he'll	he will
she'll	she will
can't	can not
don't	do not

doesn't	does not
won't	will not
couldn't	could not
shouldn't	should not

These, and many other contractions as well, all stem from an understandable desire to shorten very common words, the same desire that produces "Ma" and "Pa" or nicknames.

CONTRACTIONS IN WRITING

One of the differences between speech and writing is in the use of contractions. The more formal the writing, the fewer the contractions. Everyday speech is quite informal, while most college writing is more formal. That means you would be wise to limit your use of contractions in your writing, particularly when you are treating a subject formally, as in a book report or a research paper. The best advice is to save the bulk of your contractions for those occasions when you want to talk in an informal manner.

Another important point is that if you use contractions sparingly, you will have fewer difficulites with confusing "there," "their," and "they're" or "your" and "you're," as well as "its" and "it's."

PROBLEMS WITH CONTRACTIONS

your/you're

Think of the clear difference between "were" and "we're":

were	the past of the verb "is," related to something that has already happened
we're	contraction meaning "we are"

So far, so good—but look at the next example:

your	shows ownership: "Is that your car?"
you're	a contraction meaning "you are": "You're kidding."

This is one of the most troublesome contractions in English. Make sure you know the differences by heart.

EXERCISE 1

Underline the correct word in the following sentences:
1. Where are your/you're gloves?
2. As long as your/you're up, get me some soda.
3. Who is your/you're doctor?
4. Are you sure your/you're well enough to walk?

5. When your/you're in Florida, look for your/you're sister.
6. Doesn't that man have your/you're coat?
7. I certainly don't want to meet any of your/you're friends.
8. Make sure you watch where your/you're going.
9. Is that the car your/you're driving nowadays?
10. I'm afraid your/you're sitting on your/you're hat.

Remember: "your" shows ownership; it is a possessive pronoun (see the chart on page 157). "You're" means "you are." The apostrophe has nothing to do with possession.

EXERCISE 2

Write three sentences using *both* "your" and "you're" in *each*. Use sentence five in Exercise 1 as an example.

1. _____

_____

2. _____

_____

3. _____

_____

its/it's

Think of the clear difference between "his" and "he's":

his   shows ownership: "Where is his house?"
he's   a contraction meaning "he is": "Who does he think he's fooling?"

The difference between "his" and "he's" is exactly the same as the difference between "its" and "it's":

its   shows ownership: "The dog lost its bone."
it's   a contraction meaning "it is": "It's late."

"Its" can be confusing. The word refers to possession or ownership in the same way that "his" or "her" does:

The man broke his leg. (leg belongs to man—his)
The woman broke her leg. (leg belongs to woman—her)
The doll broke its leg. (leg belongs to doll—its)

"Its" shows that a thing or an object owns something else:

The moon has lost its glow.
The wind has increased its strength.
The cat found its toy. (Animals can be "he," "she," or "it.")

EXERCISE 3

Underline the correct word in the following sentences:
1. I'm unhappy because its/it's raining.
2. Did you give the parrot its/it's food?
3. Look and see if its/it's leg is better.
4. Look and see if its/it's still cloudy outside.
5. You're lucky its/it's not broken.
6. I know its/it's late, but its/it's our anniversary.
7. Do you know whether its/it's dangerous?
8. The car lost one one of its/it's hubcaps.
9. Its/it's my birthday.
10. The team seemed to lose its/it's spirit.

Remember:

1. "It's" *always* means "it is." The apostrophe has nothing to do with possession.
2. "Its" *always* shows ownership. It doesn't need an apostrophe because it is a possessive pronoun, just like "his" or "her."
3. When you use "it's," always see if you can substitute "it is." If the sentence makes no sense with "it is," then you know you need "its" instead.

EXERCISE 4

Write three sentences using *both* "its" and "it's" in each. *Example:* Although the leaves are missing, its bark shows that it's a maple.

1. _____

_____

2. _____

_____

3. _____

_____

they're/there/their

The word "they're" would cause no trouble by itself, but "there" and "their" sound like it and are often confused with it.

they're a contraction meaning "they are": "They're all leaving the party."
their shows ownership; it is the plural of "his," "her," and "its": "They lost their heads."
there 1. a place, the opposite of "here": "Sit over there."
    2. introduces ideas and sentences: "There are fifty states."

Examples
1. My cousins said <u>they're</u> going to Hawaii. (THEY ARE)
2. Why are you sitting <u>there</u>? (A PLACE)
3. <u>There</u> is a full moon tonight. (INTRODUCING AN IDEA)
4. My neighbors all mow <u>their</u> lawns. (OWNERSHIP)

EXERCISE 5

Underline the correct word in the following sentences:
1. Where there/their/they're is smoke there/their/they're is fire.
2. The birds all flew out of there/their/they're cages.
3. They say there/their/they're not going to the game.
4. Who is that woman over there/their/they're?
5. Why did they all leave there/their/they're coats?
6. Mr. Sanchez used to live in the house there/their/they're now re-building.
7. Unless there/their/they're masters called them, the dogs wouldn't respond.
8. I told him that there/their/they're didn't seem to be any motive for the crime.
9. When did they get there/their/they're new car?
10. Are you sure there/their/they're house is big enough?

EXERCISE 6

Write three sentences using *both* "there" and "they're" in *each*. *Example:* <u>They're</u> sitting over <u>there</u>.

1. _____

_____

2. _____

_____

3. _____

_____

EXERCISE 7

Write three sentences using *both* "their" and "they're" in *each*. *Example:* <u>They're</u> in <u>their</u> own cars.

1. _____

_____

2. _____

_____

3. _____

_____

EXERCISE 8

Write three sentences using *all three* (there, their, they're) in *each*.
Example: <u>They're</u> out <u>there</u> on <u>their</u> surfboards.

1. _____

_____

2. _____

_____

3. _____

_____

EXERCISE 9

Finish the following ten sentences. They will all have the same form;
you must keep the comma. *Examples:*
    Whenever its <u>engine is cold, the car runs poorly.</u>
        ("its" refers to the thing that owns the engine.)
    Whenever it's <u>cold, the car runs poorly.</u>
        ("it's" refers to the weather; it means "it is.")

1. Since there _____,

_____.

2. Since their _____,

_____.

3. Since they're _____,

_____.

4. While your _____,

_____.

5. While you're _____,

_____.

6. Until it's _____,

_____.

7. Until its _____,

_____.

8. Although there _____,

_____.

9. Although their _____,

_____.

10. Although they're _____,

_____.

EXERCISE 10

Finish the following ten sentences. They will all have the same form;
you must keep the comma. *Examples:*
  Because your <u>book is missing, you should borrow another.</u>
    ("your" shows ownership; "you" have the book)
  Because you're <u>responsible for the book, be careful.</u>
    ("you're" means "you are")

1. If you're _____,

_____.

2. If your _____,

_____.

3. When it's _____,

_____.

4. When its _____,

_____.

5. Because there _____,

_____.

6. Because their _____,

_____.

7. After they're _____,

_____.

8. After it's their _____,

_____.

9. If they're your _____ ,

_____ .

10. If you're their _____ ,

_____ .

Summary

contraction	possessive pronoun
it's = it is	its = belonging to it
you're = you are	your = belonging to you
they're = they are	their = belonging to them

there $\begin{cases} 1. \text{ a place, as in "over there"} \\ 2. \text{ introduces sentences and ideas} \end{cases}$

Homonyms

Words that sound the same but have different spellings and meanings are called *homonyms*. They run in pairs or trios, and because they sound the same they are often confused in writing. This section lists the most common problems with homonyms. Remember that the pairs of words here are all pronounced the same, though the spellings and meanings are always different.

brake/break

BRAKE (noun)   the device that stops a vehicle (She slammed on the <u>brake</u> pedal. This bus has new <u>brakes</u>.)

BREAK (noun) $\begin{cases} \text{a favor (Give me a } \underline{break}. \text{ INFORMAL)} \\ \text{a pause (Take a } \underline{break}.) \end{cases}$

BREAK (verb)   to crack or split (Don't <u>break</u> your leg.)

EXERCISE 11

Fill in the right word, break/brake:

1. The company developed a new type of _____.

2. She wants to _____ the world record.

3. Did you _____ the tennis racket?

4. It was just a lucky _____.

5. It's time to _____ for lunch.

6. Did you check the _____?

7. In Monte Carlo he tried to _____ the bank.

8. There was a short _____ in the action.

9. Didn't that _____ the window?

10. Larry thought he could _____ into advertising.

EXERCISE 12

Write six sentences: two for "brake," two for "break" as a noun, and two for "break" as a verb.

1. _____

_____

2. _____

_____

3. _____

_____

4. _____

_____

5. _____

_____

6. _____

clothes/close

CLOTHES (noun)   garments (We bought new <u>clothes</u>.)

(Clothing is made of CLOTH, as are towels and upholstery. The plural of CLOTH is CLOTHS, as in table<u>cloths</u> and dish<u>cloths</u>.)

CLOSE (verb)   { shut, finish (<u>Close</u> the door.)
{ get near (Night <u>closed</u> in.)

(The descriptive word (adjective) CLOSE means "near" or "intimate." It is not pronounced like the verb: They were very <u>close</u> friends.)

EXERCISE 13

Fill in the right word, close/clothes:

1. Where did you get those _____?

2. Who can _____ that window?

3. They managed to _____ the gap.

4. They managed to find their _____.

5. Please be sure to _____ the furnace door.

EXERCISE 14

Write two sentences for "clothes" and two sentences for "close" (the verb).

1. _____

_____

2. _____

_____

3. _____

_____

4. _____

_____

know/no
knew/new

KNOW (verb)	to understand, be aware of (I <u>know</u> it. I <u>knew</u> it. I have <u>known</u> it for years.)
NO	the opposite of yes (There was <u>no</u> answer.)
NOW	rhymes with "how"—means "at present" (I want it <u>now</u>.)
KNEW (verb)	past of KNOW (I <u>knew</u> it.)
NEW	up to date; not old (She has a <u>new</u> coat.)

Use of these words will become clearer when you master KNOW's various parts: know; knew; known; knowing.

EXERCISE 15

Write two sentences, using *all three* words (know, now, no) in *each*. *Example:* <u>Now</u> I <u>know</u> why <u>no</u> wine was served.

1. _____

2. _____

EXERCISE 16

Write two sentences using *both* "knew" and "new" in *each*. *Example:*
They <u>knew</u> I wanted a <u>new</u> skirt.

1. _____

2. _____

EXERCISE 17

Fill in the right word: know, no, now, knew, new:

1. I _____ they wouldn't be here by _____.
2. They all _____ he can't afford a _____ house.
3. Does anyone _____ the answer?
4. There has never been a better time than _____.
5. She acts like she _____ them.
6. There are four _____ facts you need to _____.
7. It's _____ business of yours.
8. When I _____ him he was a _____ student at school.
9. They wish they _____ who set the fire.
10. Until _____ I never _____ who lived in that _____ house.

passed/past

PASSED (verb) gone by; part of PASS (Did he <u>pass</u> the test? Yes, he <u>passed</u>.)
PAST   before now; former (The <u>past</u> is always with us. This <u>past</u> year I had a job.)

EXERCISE 18

Fill in the right word: pass/passed/past.

1. He hasn't _____ a single subject.
2. A huge bird just _____ overhead.

3. His aunt has never looked better these _____ weeks.

4. The _____ president applauded her successor.

5. Larry was always _____ over for raises.

6. I hope I can _____ the examination.

7. I hope I have _____ the examination.

8. I am glad that examination time has _____.

9. The _____ has always fascinated Janet.

10. By now a whole year must have _____ since the wedding.

EXERCISE 19

Write two sentences, using *both* "past" and "passed" in *each*. *Example:*
In the past, my three cousins passed every test they took.

1. _____

_____

2. _____

_____

patience/patients

PATIENCE (noun)   ability to wait (Cooking well takes patience.)
PATIENTS (noun)   people who see a doctor (singular, PATIENT)
                Dr. Kelly saw one patient.
                Dr. Kelly saw two patients.

The descriptive word (adjective) PATIENT means "able to wait" (He was very patient). A person who is PATIENT possesses the virtue of PATIENCE.

EXERCISE 20

Fill in the correct word, patience/patients:

1. The job required more _____than he possessed.

2. Only _____ with serious disabilities should call on Monday.

3. If you want an example of _____, look at a spider.

4. They had to hire a new, more careful watchman, because some of
the _____ complained.

5. Doctors make terrible _____ because they never follow anyone's
advice.

EXERCISE 21

Write two sentences using "patients" and two more sentences using "patience." Then write two sentences using *both* words in *each* one.

1. _____

_____

2. _____

_____

3. _____

_____

4. _____

_____

5. _____

_____

6. _____

_____

principal/principle

PRINCIPAL (noun)	the person in charge of a school (The school had a terrific principal.)
PRINCIPAL (descriptive word)	most important (His principal motive was greed.)
PRINCIPLE (noun)	basic truth or belief (She had strong principles. It was a fundamental principle.)

EXERCISE 22

Fill in the right word, principal/principle:

1. I could never figure out how they hired the new _____.

2. It takes study to understand the _____ of chemical bonding.

3. She decided that the government had lost track of the most important _____.

4. The _____ reason for the accident was a broken gas main.

5. Was it a subsidiary motive or a _____ one?

EXERCISE 23

Write six sentences: two for the noun "principal," two for the noun "principle," and two for the descriptive word "principal."

1. _____

_____

2. _____

_____

3. _____

_____

4. _____

_____

5. _____

_____

6. _____

_____

to/too/two

TWO	the number 2
TO	toward, in the direction of (Let's go to the park.)
	before verbs (infinitive) (I want to go home.)
TOO	also, as well as (They have too much.)
	more than enough, to a great extent (It was too close for comfort.)

This last use of TOO is a major problem area. The word gets written "to" when it should be "too much" or "too many." Think of it this way:

It was too good to be true.
$$\begin{cases} \text{too good} = \text{more than enough} = O + O \\ \text{to be} = \text{before a verb} = \text{one O} \end{cases}$$

EXERCISE 24

Fill in the correct word, to/too/two:

1. Which store did they send her _____?

2. Manuel is more patient than his _____ brothers.

3. Are you sure you're not _____ tired?

4. When I get home, I'm going ———— sleep for ———— hours.

5. Tell them ———— stop in ———— see me.

6. It's ———— hot ———— stay indoors.

7. The farmers harvested ———— much hay, so they sold the excess ———— the commune.

8. Are you thirsty ————?

9. Are you ready ———— swim?

10. She thought it ———— far ———— walk.

EXERCISE 25

Write three sentences, using *all three* words (to, two, too) in *each. Examples:* Her <u>two</u> sisters want <u>to</u> go <u>too</u>. We're <u>too</u> late <u>to</u> see the <u>two</u> movies.

1. _____

_____

2. _____

_____

3. _____

_____

EXERCISE 26

Correct the following sentences by crossing out the wrong word and writing in the proper word above:

1. Two miles is to far to walk.

2. Are you sure you want too go to?

3. Every too miles she claimed they were going to far.

4. Why did you say it was two late?

5. There were to many people two cook for, so they went to the restaurant for some take-out food.

weather/whether

WEATHER (noun)   climate (Here is the <u>weather</u> forecast.)
WHETHER   indicates alternatives (I don't know <u>whether</u> I'm coming or going.)

EXERCISE 27

Fill in the correct word, weather/whether:

1. They asked _____ they could use the pool.

2. Since the _____ was fine, the girls walked home.

3. Cats stay in when the _____ is bad.

4. _____ you come or not is up to you.

5. It's all a question of _____ you want to or not.

EXERCISE 28

Write three sentences, using *both* "weather" and "whether" in *each*.
Example: <u>Whether</u> I go or stay depends on the <u>weather</u>.

1. _____

_____

2. _____

_____

3. _____

_____

which/witch

WHICH	what one or the one (<u>Which</u> seat is yours?)
WITCH (noun)	evil old woman (She is a <u>witch</u>.)

EXERCISE 29

Fill in the correct word, which/witch:

1. There were so many he didn't know _____ one to pick.

2. The children thought they saw a _____.

3. The bus, _____ was full of passengers, passed us by.

4. _____ book were you reading?

5. I don't know _____ question to answer first.

EXERCISE 30

Write three sentences using "which" and three sentences using "witch."

1. _____

_____

2. _____

_____

3. _____

_____

4. _____

_____

5. _____

_____

6. _____

_____

CONFUSING CONTRACTIONS

Some of the most common contractions sound just the same as other words, so they could also be called homonyms. The most troublesome ones are:

IT'S	it is (<u>It's</u> snowing.)
ITS	belonging to it (The paint lost <u>its</u> shine.)
LET'S	let us (<u>Let's</u> climb that hill.)
LETS	allows (He <u>lets</u> everyone use his phone.)
THEY'RE	they are (<u>They're</u> out.)
THEIR	belonging to them (They took <u>their</u> seats.)
THERE	a place (Put it <u>there</u>.)

There is no contraction for THERE ARE. (<u>There's</u> my brother. <u>There are</u> my brothers.)

WHO'S	who is (<u>Who's</u> the principal of this school?)
WHOSE	belonging to someone (She is the woman <u>whose</u> house burned down.)
YOU'RE	you are (<u>You're</u> not serious.)
YOUR	belonging to you (Remember <u>your</u> manners.)

Look-Alikes

The words in this section are not homonyms, for they do not have the same sound. Nevertheless, they sound and look similar enough to cause confusion. They are presented in pairs, with only the major meanings given.

accept/except

ACCEPT (verb)	to receive (I <u>accept</u> the suggestion. He <u>accepts</u> praise well. She <u>accepted</u> the gift.)
EXCEPT	other than (She saw every hat <u>except</u> her own.)

EXERCISE 31

Fill in the correct word, accept/except:

1. One of the directors will _____ the award.

2. Harry found it hard to _____ criticism.

3. Everyone came _____ my brother.

4. Everyone came to _____ my brother.

5. Everyone who knows her _____ her.

EXERCISE 32

Write two sentences each for "accept" and "except."
Accept

1. _____

_____

2. _____

_____

Except

3. _____

_____

4. _____

_____

advice/advise

ADVICE (noun)	recommendation (That's good <u>advice</u>. What <u>advice</u> do you have? I need some <u>advice</u>.)
ADVISE (verb)	to recommend, warn, to give advice (What boots do you <u>advise</u>? She <u>advises</u> her patients to avoid fried food. I <u>advised</u> him about his finances.)

When you give <u>advice</u> it is called <u>advising</u> and you are an <u>adviser</u>.

EXERCISE 33

Fill in the correct word, advice/advise:

1. What type of _____ is this?

2. He spent the day giving _____ on the new laws.

3. What did they _____?

4. What kind of _____ did they give?

5. Did you _____ them of the label's warning?

EXERCISE 34

Write two sentences for each.
Advice

1. _____

   _____

2. _____

   _____

Advise

3. _____

   _____

4. _____

   _____

choose/chose

These are parts of the same verb, which means "to pick" or "to select."

CHOOSE	present (Don't <u>choose</u> up sides. You always <u>choose</u> the hard way.)
CHOSE	past (They <u>chose</u> up sides. He <u>chose</u> a number.)
CHOSEN	compound form; past participle (We have <u>chosen</u> poorly. A few are never <u>chosen</u>.)

Remember: the present, CHOOSE, has two O's; the past, CHOSE, has one.

EXERCISE 35

Fill in the correct word, choose/chose:

1. I wish he'd _____ a different dessert.

2. Martin _____ to stay home.

3. Which gift did they _____? They _____ a mirror.

4. When they have ice cream they all _____ strawberry.

5. I'm afraid I _____ a bad time to arrive.

EXERCISE 36

Write six sentences: two for "choose," two for "chose," and two for "chosen."

Choose

1. _____

_____

2. _____

_____

Chose

3. _____

_____

4. _____

_____

Chosen

5. _____

_____

6. _____

_____

loose/lose

LOOSE	unattached; the opposite of tight (Is that seatbelt too loose?)
LOSE (verb)	to be unable to find; opposite of win (He is trying to lose weight. She never loses at poker. They lost their places.)

When you lose something, you have a LOSS: "It was a total loss."

EXERCISE 37

Fill in the correct word, loose/lose:

1. Pamela preferred _____, flowing clothes.

2. They always suspected he would _____.

3. The doctor advised him to ――――― weight and wear ―――――
clothing.

4. He didn't want to ――――― the race, so he made sure his muscles
were ―――――.

5. Jose was sure he had nothing to ―――――.

EXERCISE 38

Write eight sentences: two for "loose," two for "lose," two for "lost,"
and two for "loss."

Loose

1. ――

――

2. ――

――

Lose

3. ――

――

4. ――

――

Lost

5. ――

――

6. ――

――

Loss

7. ――

――

8. ――

――

quiet/quite

QUIET (two syllables) peaceful (It is a quiet town.)
QUITE (one syllable) very, rather (It is quite late.)

EXERCISE 39

Fill in the correct word, quite/quiet:

1. The music stopped, leaving the valley _____.

2. The music stopped, leaving the valley _____ and calm.

3. The music stopped, leaving the valley _____ calm.

4. I always knew he was the _____ type.

5. The paint job is not _____ good enough.

EXERCISE 40

Write four sentences: two using "quiet" and two using "quite."
Quiet

1. _____

_____

2. _____

_____

Quite

3. _____

_____

4. _____

_____

raise/rise

RAISE (verb)	to lift something up; always followed by the object being lifted. (He <u>raises</u> his hand. His aunt <u>raises</u> celery. We'll <u>raise</u> the orphans ourselves.)
RISE (verb)	to go up (Bread <u>rises</u>. The sun <u>rose</u>. They have already <u>risen</u>.)

If it acts on its own, use RISE; if someone makes it happen, use RAISE.

RAISE (noun)	an increase in pay (The boss gave her employees a big <u>raise</u>.)
RISE (noun)	an increase as in elevation (There was a <u>rise</u> in their standard of living.)

EXERCISE 41

Fill in the correct word, raise/rise:

1. She can _____ seven children all by herself.

2. Won't anyone _____?

3. Won't anyone _____ a hand?

4. Use a jack to _____ the car to the proper level.

5. The _____ in prices is due to inflation.

6. Will the fish _____ to the bait?

7. The workers angrily demanded a _____.

8. He was shocked to see so many people _____ objections.

9. Around here the sun _____ early.

10. In order to _____ in the world, he went to school.

set/sit

SET (verb)	to place, to put down, to arrange (I'll <u>set</u> this box here. She <u>sets</u> her plants in rows. They all <u>set</u> their clocks.)
SIT (verb)	to take a seat (I'll <u>sit</u> over here. He <u>sits</u> in his chair all day. They <u>sat</u> down to dinner.)

SET is usually followed by the thing that is being placed or arranged.
    Some speakers use phrases like "setting around" or "I set myself down." Writing requires SIT or SAT: "sitting around" and "I sat down."

EXERCISE 42

Fill in the correct word, sit/set:

1. Henry _____ himself a difficult task.

2. The patients used to _____ quietly.

3. Where should they _____?

4. Where should they _____ the chair?

5. My advice is to _____ and study the chart again.

EXERCISE 43

Write four sentences, two using "sit," and two using "set."
Sit

1. _____

    _____

2. _____

    _____

Set

3. _____

   _____

4. _____

   _____

than/then

THAN	used in comparisons (It's later <u>than</u> you think. I'm taller <u>than</u> he is.)
THEN	at that time (<u>Then</u> what did you do? I was thinner <u>then</u>.)

The most common problem is using THEN in place of THAN. Recall a few well-known expressions: more <u>than</u> you know; faster <u>than</u> a speeding bullet; more powerful <u>than</u> a locomotive.

EXERCISE 44

Fill in the correct word, then/than:

1. First turn the key; _____ step on the gas.

2. They ran much faster _____.

3. They ran much faster _____ they once did.

4. Up until _____, I earned more _____ George.

5. I got out of there quicker _____ I thought possible.

EXERCISE 45

Write six sentences: two using "than," two using "then," and two using *both* "then" and "than."

Then

1. _____

   _____

2. _____

   _____

Than

3. _____

   _____

4. _____

_____

Then *and* Than (*Example:* I'm smarter now <u>than</u> I was <u>then</u>.)

5. _____

_____

6. _____

_____

were/where

WERE (verb) the past of "are" (We <u>are</u> here; we <u>were</u> here. <u>Are</u> they? <u>Were</u> they?)

WHERE a place (Put that back <u>where</u> you found it. Give me a home <u>where</u> buffaloes roam.)

EXERCISE 46

Write six sentences: two using "where," two using "were," and two using *both* "where" and "were."

Where

1. _____

_____

2. _____

_____

Were

3. _____

_____

4. _____

_____

Where *and* Were (*Example:* <u>Where were</u> you?)

5. _____

_____

6. _____

_____

Words and Meanings

Your most reliable guide to finding out what words mean will be a good dictionary. Are there bad dictionaries? Yes. The thirty-nine cent drugstore special will never be good enough for your purposes; it's too short and the definitions aren't accurate or thorough enough. And don't be deceived into thinking that anything called Webster's will do. Anybody can use the Webster name on a dictionary; the name is no guarantee of quality.

What you will need is one of these good "college" dictionaries:

The Random House Dictionary
The American Heritage Dictionary
Webster's New World Dictionary
Merriam-Webster's New Collegiate Dictionary

These excellent books are available in hard cover; shorter versions of the last three come in paperback. Buy one and use it.

A typical entry in a dictionary looks like this:

dair'y (dar'i), n. plural, dairies. [From M.E. *deierie*, from A.S. *daege*] 1. The place where milk is made into butter or cheese. 2. A business or farm that produces or sells milk, butter, and cheese.

From this or any other entry you can learn much more than simply what the word means. An entry gives much information that will help you:

Spelling   The acceptable spelling or spellings of the word. Spelling of the plural and other forms if irregular.

Syllables   Where to break up a word if it can't fit on one line. (Words can be separated only at syllables; one-syllable words can't be separated at all. Instead of crowding all the letters into a tiny spot at the end of a line, break the word at the gap between the syllables.)

Pronunciation   Those strange-looking letters in parentheses all have a meaning. Look at the bottom of the page for a guide to the pronunciation symbols. Those symbols, together with the accent marks ('), will tell you the most common pronunciation(s) of the word.

Part of Speech   The abbreviations "n." and "v.," for instance, tell you whether the word is a noun or a verb. Some words are both, so the noun meaning and verb meaning will be given separately.

Synonyms (same meaning) and Antonyms (opposite meaning) For some words, other words with similar meanings are grouped together. Other groups have words with opposite meanings.

Meaning This, of course, is the major business of an entry. The entry will provide the word's precise meaning, along with the different shades of meaning it can take on. Dictionaries tend to give as many meanings as possible; the first is usually the most common. In some dictionaries the first meaning is the oldest.

Derivation (where the word comes from) The abbreviations ME (Middle English) and AS (Anglo-Saxon) tell you that "dairy" was originally a word in the language spoken in England over a thousand years ago. Other words came into English from other languages; the dictionary will tell the source for almost every word it lists.

Facts and Figures Most dictionaries have the following statistics: lists of common abbreviations; explanations of foreign words and phrases; names of cities, countries, and continents (with population figures); lists of famous men and women (with their dates); names of colleges.

EXERCISE 47

Look up the following words in your dictionary and be able to (1) pronounce them, (2) spell them, and (3) define them. Then write a sentence using each one in the space provided.

1. martial: _____

2. imply: _____

3. consequence: _____

4. aspire: _____

5. gourmet: _____

6. attain: _____

7. specific: _____

8. irate: _____

9. naive: _____

10. nullify: _____

Increase Your Vocabulary

The best way to increase your vocabulary is, as you know, to read books and magazines. But even if you don't become a heavy reader, here are some ways that can help you master more words:

1. When hearing or seeing a word you don't know, look it up.
2. When you find out what it means, make it your own; use it.
3. Keep a list of the words you are learning. If the spelling gives you trouble, put the word on your spelling list.

DICTION

Diction means the right choice of words. Of the huge number of words in the English language, some are more suitable for speech, some are more suitable for writing, and most are suitable for both. You will have to be aware of the words that do not appear in most formal writing, and the kinds of words that can cause any writer problems. These guidelines deal with three sets of words: slang, clichés, and vague words.

Save Slang for Speaking.   Writing usually demands a more formal diction than speaking. This doesn't mean that writing can't be informal—plenty of good writing is. But slang is almost always unsuitable for written work in school and business.

You already make a distinction between slang and more formal writing. If you're applying for a job, for instance, you might be asked to describe what your last job was like. How do you do it? Would you say "My last job was a real bummer because the old man hassled me all the time"? No. You'd write on the application "The job was difficult." Would you say "I learned lots of stuff about the business"? No. You'd say "I learned how the business operates." These distinctions are perfectly normal; you make them all the time, employing a wide variety of speaking and writing styles.

In most college writing, you'll be asked to stick to the more formal type, and it's important to avoid overusing slang. These are some words to stay away from:

cool	chick	with it	far out
busted	dude	wheels	bad (meaning good)
ripoff	guy	hassle	ain't
bummer	kid	old man	you know

Nobody uses all these terms, and new ones are being invented all the time. You probably know yourself what the latest slang terms are; they're exactly the ones to be careful about. And don't expect to make slang acceptable by putting quotation marks around it: "The job was a 'bummer'" is no better for the quotation marks.

Note: Contractions ending in 's, 'd, and 've are often considered too informal for most college writing. Use them cautiously.

Clichés   are worn-out, tired expressions used so often that they're a bore. Avoid them and your writing will be livelier and more personal. A cliché is someone else's term; think of your own and your writing will be better.

These are some of the more obvious clichés and overused expressions to watch out for:

acid test	fast and loose
face the music	feel in my bones

few and far between
giant step forward
head in the clouds
head over heels
in the same boat
know the ropes
last but not least
leaps and bounds
light as a feather

long and short of it
make no bones about it
play with fire
set one's heart on
short and sweet
skin of my teeth
today's world
true fact
walking on air

If you're tempted to use these words, remember that they have been used over and over for the past hundred years. If you can, think up another word. If you do use clichés, never put them in quotation marks.

Vague Words   are so general that they don't tell you anything. They seem to be saying something but really aren't. Writing should be clear, specific, and precise; vagueness is a serious danger, as the following sentence illustrates:

> We certainly had a very nice time. It was so much fun staying at that fabulous hotel, eating really good food, and looking at the spectacular scenery.

The student who wrote this thought she had communicated something to the reader, but did she? Do you know much after reading these two sentences? All you get is that she had a sense of pleasure. The words "nice," "so much fun," "fabulous," "good," and "spectacular" don't say enough, particularly in writing. When you say them out loud you can convey part of your meaning through your tone of voice, but you have to rely on the words themselves in writing.

Take this sentence: *Her dress was nice.* How would you say it if:

1. It was the best-looking dress you had ever seen?
2. You weren't excited by it one way or the other?
3. You wanted to be sarcastic?

There is no way to convey the different tones of voice on the page, so when you write you have to give more than a vague word like "nice."

Here are some other vague words:

a lot (*two* words)
awful
disgusting
fabulous
good
great
horrible
many

marvelous
much
quite
really
sensational
spectacular
so much
thing
very

You can't avoid all these words, but be sure that they're not used as a substitute for real description and detail. And don't think that a combination of these words will be better than any of them alone: "really nice" is just as vague as "nice."

Note: Check the section "Concrete Language" (pages 13–22) for more suggestions about the right kind of description to use.

Spelling

When it comes to spelling, a word is either right or wrong. Close doesn't count. How is your spelling? Are you fairly confident about it, or do you need some pointers? This chapter will not turn poor spellers into spelling wizards, but it can help you make a start on getting most words right.

The first point to realize is that nobody can give you *all* the rules. English spelling is often complicated and frustrating; anyone who tried to learn all the rules and exceptions would be better off putting that energy into something more useful. You can always look a word up, especially if you have a general idea of its spelling.

The next step is to understand that you have to work at improving your spelling. Teachers aren't going to spend weeks and weeks on spelling; there are more important things to do in most English classes. That means that you'll have to devise your own ways of teaching yourself. Here are five:

1. *Keep a list of the words you get wrong.* (There is room for one on the inside back cover of this book.)
2. *When you get a paper back, look over the corrections* for misspelled words. Find out how to spell the words correctly and put them down on your list.
3. *Underline the difficult letters.* Make up devices to help you keep the letters straight in your mind.
4. *Keep looking at your list.* Ask if you can bring it to exams. Refer to it when you have a spare minute or two.
5. *Get annoyed* if you keep getting the same words wrong. You have to keep at it; never think that it's hopeless. If you're willing to make the effort, the words will soon be yours—permanently. Then you'll start to cross words off the list, a very satisfying feeling.

This section gives five specific rules for spelling. They will not necessarily *solve* everything for you; they give the basic patterns and the most frequent exceptions.

SPELLING RULES

Terms

<u>Vowel</u>: A E I O U (sometimes Y)
<u>Consonant</u>: all other letters
<u>Suffix</u>: word ending. Some suffixes begin with vowels: -ed; -er; -es; -ing. Some begin with consonants: -ly; -ment; -ness; -ful.

THE BASIC FORMULA

Most English words are regular; that is, you simply add the ending, called a "suffix."

walk, walk<u>s</u>, walk<u>ed</u>, walk<u>er</u>, walk<u>ing</u>
rest, rest<u>s</u>, rest<u>ed</u>, rest<u>ing</u>
girl, girl<u>s</u>

Some words make certain changes when adding suffixes; the most common changes are covered in these rules.

Rule 1

Add -es instead of -s
A. When an extra syllable is pronounced. *Examples:* church, church<u>es</u>; fox, fox<u>es</u>
B. When a noun ends in -o preceded by a consonant. *Examples:* potato, potato<u>es</u>; hero, hero<u>es</u>; veto, veto<u>es</u> (A major exception is for words taken from Italian. *Examples:* soprano<u>s</u>, piano<u>s</u>, solo<u>s</u>; all are regular.)

Rule 2

Change final -y to -i before adding a suffix when -y is preceded by a consonant. *Examples:* berry, berr<u>ies</u>; company, compan<u>ies</u>
This rule *does not apply* to the -ing ending. *Examples:* fly, fl<u>ies</u>, fly<u>ing</u>; try, tr<u>ies</u>, try<u>ing</u>

Rule 3

Drop a final -e when a suffix begins with a vowel. *Examples:* dine, din<u>ing</u>, din<u>ed</u>; give, giv<u>ing</u>; note, not<u>ing</u>; vote, vot<u>ing</u>
Keep the -e when the suffix begins with a consonant. *Examples:* live, liv<u>ing</u> (-ing begins with a vowel), lively (-ly begins with a consonant); hope, hoping, hopeful; arrange, arranging, arrangement. *Exceptions:* truly; argument

Rule 4

Put "i" before "e"
A. Except after "c." *Examples:* rec<u>ei</u>ve; dec<u>ei</u>ve
B. Or when sounded like "a." *Examples:* n<u>ei</u>ghbor; w<u>ei</u>gh   *Exceptions:* some "ei" exceptions are written in the form of a sentence to help you remember: L<u>ei</u>sured for<u>ei</u>gn financ<u>ie</u>rs s<u>ei</u>ze w<u>ei</u>rd h<u>ei</u>ghts.

Rule 5

Double the final consonant *only* if these three conditions are met:
A. Suffix begins with a vowel. *Examples:* -ing, -er, -ed, -est

B. Word is of one syllable or last syllable is stressed. *Examples:* re fer′, o mit′

C. Word ends in *one* consonant preceded by *one* vowel. *Examples:* oc cur′, quit, split

Examples of Rule 5

shop, sho<u>pp</u>er, sho<u>pp</u>ed, sho<u>pp</u>ing (but shop<u>s</u> because of A. in Rule 5)
sin, sinned, sinner, sinning
begin, beginner, beginning

Do not double any other final letters: Some students write:

dinning for dining
shinning for shining
writting for writing

See C. in Rule 5 for why the consonants are not doubled in these words.

The following list contains words that are often misspelled. Some of them probably give you trouble. Pick out the problems you have and transfer them to your own word list.

Words Often Misspelled

Troublesome letters underlined

achi<u>e</u>ve	gramma<u>r</u>	rec<u>ei</u>ve
acr<u>o</u>ss	h<u>e</u>ight	ref<u>e</u>rence
a<u>d</u>dress	ho<u>p</u>ing	rhy<u>thm</u>
argu<u>m</u>ent	immedi<u>ate</u>ly	ridic<u>u</u>lous
athl<u>e</u>te	interest	s<u>ei</u>ze
atten<u>d</u>ance	knowle<u>d</u>ge	sensi<u>b</u>le
belief	manage<u>m</u>ent	sepa<u>r</u>ate
bene<u>f</u>it	mathe<u>m</u>atics	shin<u>i</u>ng
cal<u>e</u>ndar	m<u>ea</u>nt	simi<u>l</u>ar
consci<u>e</u>nce	necessa<u>r</u>y	sinc<u>e</u>rely
cons<u>c</u>ious	occasi<u>o</u>n	sopho<u>m</u>ore
counsel<u>o</u>r	occu<u>rr</u>ed	spee<u>ch</u>
crow<u>ded</u>	opini<u>o</u>n	ster<u>eo</u>
defi<u>n</u>ite	particular	stud<u>y</u>ing
de<u>s</u>cribe	perf<u>o</u>rmance	succ<u>ee</u>d
din<u>i</u>ng	perso<u>nn</u>el	surpr<u>i</u>se
elim<u>i</u>nate	persu<u>a</u>de	thor<u>ou</u>gh
emba<u>rr</u>ass	posse<u>ss</u>	thou<u>gh</u>
enviro<u>n</u>ment	prefe<u>rr</u>ed	thoug<u>h</u>t
exa<u>gg</u>erate	preju<u>di</u>ce	tru<u>l</u>y
exist<u>e</u>nce	pres<u>e</u>nce	unt<u>i</u>l
famil<u>i</u>ar	privi<u>l</u>ege	w<u>ei</u>rd
for<u>ei</u>gn	proba<u>b</u>ly	wom<u>a</u>n
fri<u>e</u>nd	p<u>s</u>ycho<u>logy</u>	writ<u>i</u>ng
govern<u>m</u>ent	p<u>u</u>rsue	wr<u>ea</u>th

If you have trouble with any of these words, refer back to this page. Copy the most difficult ones onto your spelling list.

The following words, all problems for some students, are treated separately; look them up or the page cited:
accept/except (206), advise/advice (206), brake/break (196), choose/chose (207), close/clothes (197), its/it's (191), knew/know (198), lets/let's (205), loose/lose (208), new/no (198), passed/past (199), patience/patients (200), principal/principle (201), quiet/quite (209), raise/rise (210), set/sit (211), than/then (212), their/there/they're (192), there's/theirs (205), to/too/two (202), whether/weather (203), which/witch (204), who's/whose (205), your/you're (190).

EXERCISE 48

Take each of the words in the following groups (A through E) and (1) add -ed, (2) add -s or -es, (3) add -ing, (4) add -er. You may have to make changes; look back at the rules if you are in doubt.

	-ed	-s or -es	-ing	-er
A. write:	(1)	(2)	(3)	(4)
contain:	(1)	(2)	(3)	(4)
train:	(1)	(2)	(3)	(4)
B. pack:	(1)	(2)	(3)	(4)
package:	(1)	(2)	(3)	(4)
install:	(1)	(2)	(3)	(4)
stop:	(1)	(2)	(3)	(4)
C. strip:	(1)	(2)	(3)	(4)
stripe:	(1)	(2)	(3)	(4)
fill:	(1)	(2)	(3)	(4)
fry:	(1)	(2)	(3)	(4)
D. cry:	(1)	(2)	(3)	(4)
pare:	(1)	(2)	(3)	(4)
observe:	(1)	(2)	(3)	(4)
count:	(1)	(2)	(3)	(4)
E. interfere:	(1)	(2)	(3)	(4)
complain:	(1)	(2)	(3)	(4)

apply: (1) —————— (2) —————— (3) —————— (4) ——————

receive: (1) —————— (2) —————— (3) —————— (4) ——————

WHEN TO SPELL OUT NUMBERS

There is a simple rule for when to spell out numbers and when to use figures.

Rule

If it takes one or two words, spell it out: twenty-six; seventeen million.
If it takes more than two words, use figures: 263; 7777.

Other cautions:

1. Never begin a sentence with a numeral: "Seven hundred forty is my favorite number." *but* "My favorite number is 740."
2. Never mix written-out numbers and figures; use figures for all of them: "They grew 200 acres of potatoes last year, but this year they grew only 185."
3. Use a hyphen between written-out numbers from twenty-one to ninety-nine. (seventy; seventy-one; one hundred seventy-one)
4. In writing an essay, write "first," "second," "third," "fourth," instead of 1st, 2nd, 3rd, 4th.

MASTERY TEST I FOR THE RIGHT WORD

Correct and rewrite the following sentences:

1. Most patience cant afford to pay for there stay at this hospital.

_____

_____

2. The rain around here never let's up during the Winter.

_____

_____

3. Its going to be hard to loose that pair of purple boots.

_____

_____

4. Mr. Wheeler is alot older then you'd guess by looking at him.

_____

_____

5. I never new why there last movie failed.

_____

_____

6. That dude with the sunglasses said their all out of pickles.

_____

_____

7. Surprisingly, the attendent choose to interpret my remark as hostile.

_____

_____

8. Who's is that knew Honda?

_____

_____

9. The principle set her down and gave her some good advise.

_____

_____

10. This passed year I discovered quiet alot about how the goverment works.

_____

_____

MASTERY TEST II FOR THE RIGHT WORD

Rewrite the following sentences correctly:

1. She never let's her kids listen to none of them knew records, because she says their to loud.

   _____

   _____

2. The neighborhood I live in has loss it's quite character do to the new thruway.

   _____

   _____

3. Set that package down and help me rise the shade.

   _____

   _____

4. Are you're cousins the one's who's car has bad breaks?

   _____

   _____

5. This book of their's has everything accept a plot.

   _____

   _____

6. The kind of cloths they word then are know out of style.

   _____

   _____

7. Unaware of the leaking hydrogen, the captain tryed to land the Zeppelin before the storm past.

   _____

   _____

8. Don't worry about witch one to choose; its there decision to make.

   _____

   _____

9. She never new weather they were kidding or not.

   _____

   _____

10. For a new desk the carpenter ordered two long boards, two cabinets to sit them on, and some formica to cover them.

    _____

    _____

Index